YOU, ME and UNCLE MIKE

Welcome to YOU, ME and UNCLE MIKE this book an eclectic journey of money and secrets of life for the young of all ages.

MONEY

How Money Works, and How Money can Work for You!

Michael Sandos

ARPress

ARPress
45 Dan Road Suite 5
Canton MA 02021

| Hotline: | 1(888) 821-0229 |
| Fax: | 1(508) 545-7580 |

Ordering Information:

Quantity sales. Special discounts are available on quantity purchases by corporations, associations, and others. For details, contact the publisher at the address above.

Printed in the United States of America.

| ISBN-13: | Paperback | 979-8-89389-471-4 |
| | eBook | 979-8-89389-472-1 |

Library of Congress Control Number: 2024918666

TABLE OF CONTENTS

Chapter 1

YOU, ME AND UNCLE MIKE

Welcome to YOU, ME and UNCLE MIKE

this book It is an eclectic journey of money and the secrets of life. Written and designed for kids of all ages. This book is to teach young of all ages how to understand the wonderful world of money, When making the a **Difference, is the Difference!**

Note: I know this isn't the correct grammatical order of words, but for this book and its purpose we will say it this way, "YOU, ME and UNCLE MIKE ." INTRODUCTION:

The basis of this book is to introduce young and old the wonderful world of money and how it works. Yes that means you, everyone of you! The unique opportunity of this book is, the reader will learn how fun the world is around them, and the many different ways we as people can understand everything from **CENTS TO COMONSENSE**.

It allows us to live a happier and more a productive life and it explains that there are no short cuts or <u>are there</u>? No you can't cut short the required steps to get certain things done or to get to certain places. But, through understanding and knowledge you can short cut the steps to get the job done quicker therefore, completing the job or reach your goals faster. You see, by learning certain basic steps you develop an understanding of how money works and you are able to save time and energy to get your goals done faster and with less problems or repercussions.

YOU, ME AND UNCLE MIKE

Telling stories:

Stories of life and comparisons of life experiences, will help you understand things throughout this book. At times I will stop and give examples. When I do this I will make a "YMUM" so you will know that I am not just drifting off and it will be a signal to you to know what is taking place and you will participate with your own creativity, understanding, and knowledge. Of course you already know that "YMUM" stands for YOU, ME and Uncle MIKE.

This "YMUM" also will tell you when we are going to cover things of life that are similar or inter-related in funny Ways.

Very Important Note: Life is like a big Tug- a- War Just like this picture you never are sure who your Pulling against. Some time it's **yourself!**

So what ever we do from here forward lets have fun. Enjoy laughing and giggling about the things this book brings to mind.

Speaking of the MIND "YMUM"

I want you to try something that will change your life. This will make your life so much easier and you will achieve so much more and get so much more out of your life. It will make you a GENIUS over night.

Multi-Tasking

Most of us want <u>more for less</u> or as they say get 2 for a nickel. so lets learn to multi-task. But lets do it to the 3rd power or compound our efforts, making more efficient use of our time, efforts and strategies. As you will see in the story thinking out side the box!

YMUM: **Your neighbor has hired you to clean her garage!**

Your neighbor Lady has hired you to clean her garage and throw her old bottles away. If she paid you $10.00 to clean her garage and throw away 100 bottles in her garage. You could get your $10.00 faster by taking a short cut! You realize that (we are spending <u>Time</u>) (and time is money!) to clean the garage and throw away the bottles. So let's cut the amount of time that it takes to get the job done and compound our efforts!

WHAT SHORT-CUT WOULD YOU TAKE?

1. Carry each bottle to the trash can a 100 yards away?
2. Carry 10 Bottles to the trash can 100 yards away?
3. Break them put them in a box and then carry them to the trash can and throw them away?
4. Roll the trash can over to the bottles and throw them away?

It's your choice, how would you handle it? Think outside the Box...

You see in life there are all kinds of choices even some that are not always right in front of you. Sometimes we need to find out more about our options first and then do what we need to get the job done! Let's take another look at what our choices are.

Multi-Tasking

Where does Multi-Tasking really start and come from..

> *So lets learn to how to multi-task. But lets do it to the 3rd power or compound our efforts, Most people only use the left side of their brain. I would like you to use both sides the left and the right side of your brain making more efficient use time, efforts and strategies You will learn to multi-task in the true and highest manor using the **Right and Left side** of your brain. If you do your ability to understand and problem solve will be **Genius**. **Yes you will develop to be a genius virtually over night by using the left and right brain.***

Ok here's how you do it. I want you to simply tell yourself that you want your right side of your brain to participate in all your brain functions, thinking, problem solving In everyone of your daily functions.

You see until your right side of the brain is told what to do, it will not and can not do anything with out your command. Your right side of the brain is supportive. It Is your creative side so to make it work you simply have to relax and be real calm Telling it what you want it to do. Say things like I want my right side of my brain to assist the left side of the brain in every thing it does. To assist it in all functions And that with each and every breath you take it makes you happier, and happier And feeling better that you ever have before. Tell it that you are in perfect health And feel better than ever before.

And for now that's all it takes is to repeat this to yourself and believe in yourself And your brain will do the rest for you. One more thing while you do this lets say every morning and every night when your in bed. I want you to take a deep breath Inhaling through your nose and exhaling through your mouth.

And while you exhale tell your right side of the brain to participate and you feel better and better happier and healthier than ever before.

Now I know that sounds like a lot, but you can be anything you wish, you just need to believe in yourself. And tell yourself what you want and it will happen. So tell yourself you wish to be the very best you can and if you believe your brain will make it happen. If you need help reading, or understanding, or understanding math, or Getting your home work done. No matter what you want your right side of the brain Will make it happen. Just Believe!!

Working Smarter not Harder

Let's use some sense, with common sense And compound our interest!

We understand that the $10.00 for the job was a great deal for you and the lady, and you understood that you could get some interest on your money simply by knowing that the bottles were worth .05 cents each at the store. You could compound your money simply be taking a box and wagon, put the bottles in and take them over to the store and collect your .05 cents return on each of the bottles making an additional $5.00 for your knowledge and effort.

That's a 50% increase on your pay or a 50% return on your investment.

You turned a $10.00 job into a $15.00 gain the job was done easier, faster and better for all, the lady got her job done and you made a better deal with out charging her more.

Now you see why knowledge is Key! All of the 5 choices were great, and would have got the job done! Only one of the 5 was just a bit better choice. Your life will be filled with choices and the sooner you learn how to make those choices and to how to think out side the box. The happier you will be and the easier and more successful Your life will be.

IT's THE SAMETHING BUT ONLY DIFFERENT...

> **Are you working Hard for your Money? Or Is your Money working Hard for you?**

Putting the pieces together.

Let's let your money work **hard** for you! We can take the money and put it into the bank savings or Mutual fund and make some money on the money. While you are waiting to spend the money, use it to making more money called investment leverage your money!

Now Let's Maximize our Efforts and Create a steady stream of Money.

If you were to take the box back the lady and ask her to put the bottles in the box each week and you will return each week and haul off the bottles for her and clean the garage for her. You now have created steady income for yourself on a regular basis. I think you now have the idea! You are now thinking with common sense.

Now let your efforts work for you! I call it "Don't work harder work Smarter"

You noticed that by simply looking around the neighborhood you see her neighbors need the same thing done for them. You stop by and ask them if they to would enjoy your help? You have just compounded your business. Be sure and tell the neighbors you work for their neighbor and give her as a reference. You see people like to have someone that can tell them that you do a great job and they recommend your service.

THE SAMETHING BUT ONLY DIFFERENT… A concept

I would like to explain that I will make reference to this through out the book. Your life is filled with this concept. You need to know how to deal with this concept. Many things look and sound the same, yet they are totally different. But yet many times they are very similar. Lets have some fun with this! **YMUM**

 # Money $

Money never gets sick!

Money never takes a break!

Money never goes on Vacation!

Money works the same for everyone!

Money works all the time for everyone!

Money spends the same for everyone!

Money doesn't know the difference of who is holding it or who is spending it.

Money is equally the same, yet the looks and feel of **Money** are totally different and yet they are the same. This is one of the **YMUM** times when we see how The Phrase:

THE SAME THING, BUT ONLY DIFFERENT.

So many time in life we see this, and yes sometimes it could be confusing! Let's look at some examples of this issue:

➢ Mom & Dad	➢ Cash	➢ Interest
➢ Mr. and Mrs.	➢ Money	➢ Earnings
➢ Mr. and Mrs. Smith	➢ Stocks	➢ Dividends
➢ Bob and Carol Smith	➢ Bonds	➢ Capital Gains
➢ The Smiths	➢ Investments	➢ Simple Interest
➢ The Smiths Family	➢ Mutual Funds	➢ Compound Interest

They all sound the same but yet very different!

VALUE:

Ask yourself when you buy something do you like to get something free with your purchase? Sure we all do that's called value, getting more for your money. Well we're going to have some fun with this concept and so much more.

CHOICES

Keep it under your hat!

Your life will be filled with choices. The choices that will make the difference in you life style, happiness and sadness, rich or famous, or Money is also this way, the different choices and options for saving money sounds the same and look so good. Most of the time it sounds like we will be making money hand over fist with our money. But when it's all over we didn't make as much as we had thought. If we would have made a better choice. Or looked a little closer at the choices available and the differences. Life plays these tricks on us the same way. Yet sometimes in Life it does mean the same thing but only different!

The golden goose

Don't kill the golden goose, live on the Golden Eggs!

Knowledge is King, use your tools

Parents, teachers and friends, they are great tools for knowledge!

THE WORLD OF THE SAME THING, BUT ONLY DIFFERENT.

YMUM Your mom and dad, or mother and father, or Mr. & Mrs., all of those mean the same thing but only different. If your mom was to say to your Dad Honey, or your dad called your mom honey or your mom and dad called you honey it is a name that fits everyone the same but only different. In this case the word stayed the same but the person changed. This was a word that described and made some one special. There are other things like money, many times we call it different names but it all means the same! It gives us a short-cut to what we mean or a more direct route to understanding or achievement. Other names for money are cash or dollars or bucks, capital, earnings there are so many ways to say the same thing, but only different. Another way would be if we put a word in front of or behind a word. This may change how we're using it or what we are doing with our money.

Examples:

Money Investment means we spent the money but not really, instead it means we have invested it, knowing we were looking to make additional money on our investment.

Money Return we made money on our money, we have more money on the money spent.

Saved Money means we are accumulating money, keeping it safe for a rainy day Saving money.

Ask yourself when you buy something do you like to get something free with your purchase? Sure we all do that's called value, getting more for your money. Well we're going to have some fun with this concept and so much more.

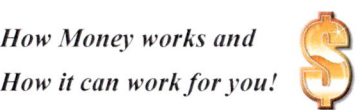
<u>Exchange Money</u> purchase also known as <u>**SPENDING MONEY**</u>

Sometimes we are doing all of them at the same time. Making money does not mean We are printing it, it means that we had a return on our money for instance an investment. Or we exchanged our US dollars for another countries money and in the exchange we made money because our US dollar was worth more.

<u>VALUE =</u> getting more out of your money. Getting 2 for a nickel.

CHOICES, CHOICES, NEVER BE IN A HURRY FOLLOW THE BASIC 10 STEPS.

Fun! Laugh! Enjoy!

MAKING MONEY = Earning more money is always more fun.

COMPOUNDING MONEY = how your money doubles at an exponential rate.

SAVING MONEY = Save on a regular basis no matter what!

EARNING MONEY = making money, one you do, the other it does.

SPENDING MONEY = We spend money to make money it all in how we do it!

MONEY RETURNS = a return on your money, cut costs and fees, reduce taxes

MONEY PROFIT = make your money work harder, while you work smarter.

MONEY MANAGEMENT = the most fun, play and to think out- side the box

SUCCESSFUL MONEY = Tax strategies keep more of your money.

SHORT MONEY = short term money is less risk more security & Safety.

LONG MONEY = long term safety with options guarantees or Assurances.

MORE MONEY = more is better, even better if it is someone else's money.

YOUR MONEY = emotionally you need to take the emotion out of your money.

TAX MONEY = Always pay the piper and you will always have sound money.

It's not what you say; It's how you say it!

As they say you need to spend it, to make it or it takes money to make money. Let your money work Hard for you, instead of you working Hard for it! Let your Money work HARDER, While You work Smarter.

Think of Money as an employee, The best employee ever it never sleeps, never gets sick, works the same for everyone, never takes a holiday or vacation, it works all the time! Sometimes we spend our money wisely and make more money by spending it!

Lets look at an example: YMUM

Let's say you earned $100.00 and you saw a bike that you wanted for a $120.00 but when you got there it on sale for $90.00 so you bought it. Let's look at what you have a $120.00 Value for an investment of $90.00 Your Investment has already made you $30.00 Just for getting what you wanted any way. The Investment made you a profit or You have equity of $30.00 (Value) Plus $ You have a balance of $ 10.00 Retained

Earnings (profit) still in your pocket. WOW!

Now if we were to sell the bike to your neighbor for the $120.00 you would have kept your $100.00 and made a profit of $30.00 total net to you, not bad for a day's work. You see your good at this and you just got started...

SYNONYMS are things that are the same, but only different. This is a great understanding of our lives. There are sayings through out the book that are simply a quick phase to give an explanation of something in a saying or phase that we hear everyday in our lives. Many times we don't understand what is being said, because we are looking at it to close, we need to relax and flow with it a bit more.

Note: Also please don't take the examples as the only view, they are just a point of view and in most cases the similarity can be viewed in many ways.

An example: I may say "don't forget to stop and smell the roses". You say what does this mean? It means don't go running through life so fast that you forgot to stop and appreciate the wonders of the world around you!

Another example is: When you were doing your homework and your mom walked by, you said, "I LOVE YOU MOM!", or your dad walked by and you said something like THANKS Dad and smiled.

<u>You just stopped and smelled the roses</u>. You stopped for just a moment to appreciate something in your life that was great and may I say you made an understanding and recognition of special people in your life that will remember your kind and great words. It's very important that you build great relationships with the right people in and through-out your life. This is one area that I love to make a part of my daily life. My favorite phrase is!

My Dad taught me everything I know, but my Mom showed me how to use it!"

My parents are my best friends. You will find your family is always there for you! Friends are many-times selective and not as willing to be there for you when the time comes.

SO BE SELECTIVE WHO YOU CALL A FRIEND.

Just like the rest of life as you will see you make it what you want! Special or Not! Remember It's up to YOU!

If you're not enjoying your family your missing a lot of fun and great learning experiences. You do realize that if you don't have a family you can always adopt one and teach them how to be quality people enjoy it's your life..

Life goes so fast, there I was riding my bike one day. Day dreaming, watching the signs go By and all of a sudden I read the sign retirement next stop! How fast do you want to go?

Are you taking advantage of the time you have and the opportunities available to you?.

Chapter 2

Most people in life are going to fast. They pass up wonderful opportunities in their lives. They simply don't know how to recognize them. They are not willing to take a few chances. Chances are a calculated risk! They need to learn to believe, to use all of their tools, apply their strategies, strengths and experiences. We will do this constantly though out this book, it's like finding $10.00 in your old pants pocket or your mom finding it!

Simple things like, knowing that if someone helps you or considers you in any way, please don't forget to show appreciation and thanks for their consideration. You may not realize that these same people may one day be the one that saves your life or would they because you could or would not take the time to say Thank You! Always show your Appreciation!

You must start from the beginning of your life to understand that our parents were your first teachers. We trusted them and they simply showed us how to use what we already knew. You see the magic computer in the sky, the Universe has all the things that have ever been or ever will be, and you already know everything there is to know. We just have to learn it, you simply have to believe in yourself or someone like your parents to guide you. They will show you how to break it down and or uncover the reality of whatever it is that you a want to learn. Simply said, you are just discovering yourself. Discovering what you already know. Give yourself a chance! What you will find is dependent on how much you can believe in yourself. Confidence is your ability to believe in yourself. It's the degree of your belief in yourself.

Making the best of what you have to work with.

- **Example: The Snow Blower Story** YMUM
- **Let's look at an example of using your tools as well as using someone else's tools to get the job done for all concerned. Mrs. Jones next door always asks you if you would shovel the snow from her walk and driveway. Her husband died and she has a rough time out in the snow & ice. And you enjoy the $10.00 dollars she gives you.**

- **Every time you finish she always has a cookie and hot chocolate ready for you in the garage. And you notice that she has a snow blower in the corner of the garage. Well you ask her does the snow blower work? Yes she says but she just can't handle it in the snow & Ice it's to hard for her. You are thinking wow if you could use that snow blower you could get a sidewalk and driveway done in less than half the time, and time is Money. So you ask her Mrs. Jones could I use her snow blower to clean the walks and driveway. You tell her will take good care of it putting gas and oil in always.**

Snow blower and
Mrs. Jones Continued

You tell her you will clean off her walk and driveway first, and then use it to do the other neighbors walks that you have been shoveling. You will then return it to her garage all cleaned off and full of gas and oil. But the best thing is that you will clean her walks and driveway off for Free. In exchange and appreciation for her letting you use it. Now you see what you have done is to use all your tools and some of others as well. If you simply apply this kind of thinking to your Money and every day life you will maximize your time and efforts. You will increase your money and save time because you are working smarter. When you think of the money you will make. Think about the same way letting your money works harder while you are working smarter.

Later you will become so confident in yourself that this process speeds up dramatically, and another things start to take place. You start to engage your othersenses to give you a much quicker and more complete answer to your search. Simply said you are now Multitasking a better use of all your tools, use of knowledge, understandings, senses, feelings, confidence, strategies, experiences both your own and others that you have learned from.

You now have the strongest power in the Universe, You believe in YOU! You will enjoy this book with Laughter, Fun, and Smiles from start to finish. The emotional side of the book is an understanding of how true life can be, and the values of life become an emotional enjoyment as a mark of success and understanding. The knowledge that you will learn is priceless. These small but great things that will simply help you be more successful through out your life. These things will help define strategies that are the wonders and the secrets that you have been missing, life and strategies. It's all about you using Strategies in your Life. If you ask it will happen, you must believe in you and your Universe. Believe In yourself...

We like the money tree grow and go through life thinking that some one is going to tell us Or show us the way. But like the tree we reach out in many directions and find our own way. But like the tree we need to have strong roots and good soil or solid in put to work with. This next section of the book will do just that for you understanding this is big time.

Chapter 3 UNDERSTANDING

People all around the world search daily trying to find answers, when the whole time it is already inside them, but they are not willing to look there. <u>How do you learn to</u> <u>believe in yourself?</u> You have to be able to look at yourself and see yourself and accept what you <u>see</u> with a <u>Smile</u>. Here's the wonderful part, you can now change and fix whatever you wish; you're in control now! It's that simple, Wow! what have you been waiting for? You now have a driver's license to go anywhere and achieve anything in your heart and mind desires. It's that simple you have been given the power.

MONEY $$$ The Money Tree You've heard "Money doesn't grow on Trees"

This is where the fun begins. We will learn the strategies of money. How money doubles is called compound interest. We will learn the difference between "simply interest vs. compound interest". We will study the strategies of how to use of both and when to use them both. We will talk about learning to negotiating, contracting and the strategies that you have been using since birth and didn't know it. You will become familiar with the different forms of currency and how taxes work, both for you and against you. The need and use of money is endless! It's all about how much you get to keep and spend.

We will also cover checkbooks, passbook savings, mutual funds, stocks, bonds and so much more. We will learn how to combine strategies for the purpose of a better program for you to use to gain success.

The Money Tree

- How to pick funds and the different charges, fees and expenses that you really need to know to use of these items in you favor. We will learn the secrets the wealthy use and why! **Let your Money work Hard for You!**

- We will study the effects of money, and how money effects people differently based on they're understanding and use of it. Something to consider would be if you're using money for you or if the money is yours or if it is someone else's, makes a great deal of difference. Your attitude of your expression of money is greatly changed depending on this concept.

- Understanding the importance of money in our lives, the uses and effects of how it changes our life is based on what we want and how we go about getting it. We think in the terms of how our life could be or would be based on money. The more we understand about it the better we will be in our choices of how to use it and how to control it. **Understanding effects that money has on people.** The use of money may change the relationships of people in and around your life. To understand the proper use of money vs. the waste and neglect of it.

One day God meet with a man, a great man very successful and wise. God told him well done you use your abilities of **confidence and belief** *to succeed. These are so important that . I must hide them so they will not be abused by man. But where those with true honor can find them, where they will be safe and no one abuse them. The man said I know in the deepest sea or ocean my lord. No said God, man will search and search and surly find it there. The man said I know in the deepest cavern in the earth no one would look there. And God replied but man is so curious he will venture there as well. Again the man said lord put them on top of the highest peaks. God said No as man wonders he will find them. I know said God I will hide them in the Hearts of man for he surely would not look in himself for the true power and Secrets of the world....You already have all the power to succeed look within yourself!*

Chapter 4

Lets look at an example; The fact of having 50% full or 50% empty. A simple concept that can make a tremendous difference to a person. Look at things as half full and not half empty! When used with money, to have a 40% discount vs. a 60% discount changes everything. But think if your on a trip your half way there not half way not there. In life were on our way always look at the positive side of things and address the negative side with gentle balance and acceptance. You see it's just like a ball half of it is positive and half is negative you need both side to complete the ball so it can roll. Your life is the same you need and have both in you it's up to you how your going to control and guide the balance.

Who am I? I am hopefully going to be your friend and Uncle Mike. Now here is **YMUM**, the fun part of the book. If you were to say **YOU ME and Uncle Mike** you are speaking about someone. When I say it, I am speaking of you, and when you say it you are speaking of me, how much fun can we have with this. We will have a great deal of fun with this concept because money is full of the same things but only different. It's like saying no one gave me a chance. But think about it, is that really true? Your mother and father gave you the blessing of life. You have been blessed with the opportunity to do with it what you want! What are you going to do with your chance? What is life worth? It's your life, your chance, your appreciation, what value, are you going to give it.

Seeing is believing, or is it?

Seeing is believing, or is it?

Sometimes life seems confusing because of the basic structure of things in our lives. It can be so much fun to play with and understand how to use this concept it can make all the difference in having fun in life. It's how you look at it…Your Perception! Your point of view! The fun of these words you, me, I, they, them, us, our, we, I, is to understand how we are all of these words depends on how we use them, they are the same, but only different. We include others in a simple word or gesture. Money is the same way we all become apart of each other in life because of money and these simple words work very much the same.

- **An example:** How to make more money on your money.

- How to make it last longer or while you have it in your possession.

- How to keep more of your money. Keep it from taxes, use of compound interest, or using simple interest when paying money, so we pay less money.

- How to buy or trade or barter another form of money usage.

- Things like this will be a part of your life from birth to death. When do you think would be a good time to understand money and how it works?

- I would say the sooner the better, wouldn't you agree? I get such a kick out of you

- and I = Us, and if you would say we and we would be refer to as

- YOU, Me and Uncle Mike as them, this is like a language of its own.

Money has some fun things that take place. If we use some of these concept discounts, to negotiate, to balance things it helps you keep track of what and where our money is and what is it doing. You need to understand that schools teach us many things, like how to count, or learning, to count our money and how to keep track of your money, and / or how to track how we are using it. But they don't show you in school how money works or how it doubles or how to balance your check book, investing, taxation and so many other things. I will show you how to understand and use these things in your daily life. I will explain that there are costs, fees, charges, and taxes that make a difference to what we call the "bottom line," which means when it is all over how much did you keep and spend.

YMUM Many people call this VALUE. We refer to money as VALUE, sometimes money increases in value and sometimes it decreases in value. The value of money in your life will be called the cost of Living or Inflation.

This either makes your money less or more valuable. When we know that a dollar bill is worth a dollar, but because of inflation it's only is worth .86 cents. In other words the dollar isn't really worth a dollar and doesn't have the buying power that we think. You see over time the cost of things increase from one year to another and the cost of an item could change by any amount for many reasons. If a stamp in 1951 cost 5 cents and today the same stamp costs 39 cents, the value of the stamp increased yet the value of the dollar decreased. Simply said, the dollar is not able to buy as much today as it did in years past this is called inflation. Maybe the costs to make the stamp have increased or decreased. What dose this have to do with you and your money? It's simple, it's simple if you put your money in a can under your bed and save it so you will have money later on in life to live on. You will loose because your money will not grow in value in the can. 30 years later your money

is worth less, than if you would have put it in a mutual fund or even the bank. You see the cost of living keeps going up and the value of your cash money goes down this is called inflation. Therefore you need your money to grow with you and with the cost of ling that increases daily.

Example: If you put a $100.00 in a can under the bed every month for 30 years, you would find that in 30 years you would have $100 X 12 months =$1200 X 30 years = $36,000. But due to inflation your $36,000 won't have the same buying power. Things 30 years later because of inflation will cost more because taxes, cost of living, keep going up and your money is still the same only worth $36,000. If we were to calculate what it is now worth you would need $69,994 to equal true value 30 years later due to a 4% inflation rate over the past 30 years. Let have some fun with this and see How easy it is to make a bunch of money with very little effort. Your $100.00 month X 12 months = $1200X 30 years = $36,000.00 if you would have invested it in a mutual fund or bank.

Your $100.00 month X 4% interest X 12 month X 30 years of compounded interest you would have in $69,994 in 30 years. Now your money has kept up with inflation and you have simply keep your value. You can see you can't just sit and wait and expect your money to keep up with life, you have to get involved learn, and understand how money works.

Lets put it All Together

Example: If you were to invest your $100 per month in a fund that gave you 6% in stead of 4% your value would be $100,562.01. But, look at if you were to get the national average interest of 12% in that same 30 years your $100.00 would be worth

$324,351.13. Now you would realistically have enough to live on for retirement. You can see the value of money if invested right makes a great deal of difference. We will come back to this in a moment.

YMUM, LETS TALK VALUE Things of value, you see it's all up to you. You make things valuable or not, you must understand Value. You can make yourself more valuable or not, both through the value of money or through the value of your opinion of yourself. Your opinion of yourself and others is what we make it. What value do we put of ourselves? Give yourself more credit and put more value on yourself. You're worth so much more than you know. Simply respect yourself and believe in yourself, sometimes we need to believe in others to learn to believe in ourselves.

To build the confidence, comfort, knowledge to believe in ourselves we start with belief in others. Looking at your parents even though they may not see things the way you do. You must understand your parents did see things the way you do at one time, years ago. when they were your age. You need to give them and yourself more value.

Respect it goes a long way!

Invest into your parents give then your confidence, and they will become more valuable to you. Give them more value, negotiate with them on the same playing field. Show them respect and you will get respect in return. It's your investment in them. Believe me you will compound your interest if you do so! Also a quick note on school and teachers! Be sure to make them special, your school, learning, and your teachers can make your world turn. They can help make your life positive with knowledge. Look at your likeness in a mirror then look at them with confidence they in turn will look at you with confidence just like a mirror when they were your age. You need to give them and yourself more value. Give them a break, have you ever been in a spot that you were trying to help and all of a sudden you were right but wrong all at the same time. Parents get into that spot all the time. They see you growing but not sure they want to except that your are a person that needs to take control and grow and do things your way. And the hard part is your way is right. You see they are right and you are right the same thing but only different. But give them some space or in their terms a time out so they can think about it and see you need to be given a chance to grow and show. It's your investment in them. Believe and give them and you a chance to flip them over to your point of view

School, Numbers, Teachers.

It's important that you understand that some things are the same but only different.

1+1=2 or 1x2=2 or 1 to the second power =2 2+2=4 or 2x2=4
3+3=6 or 2x3=6
4+4=8 or 2x4=8
Learn to use your Tools!

5+5=10 or 2x5=10
6+6=12 or 2x6=12
7+7=14 or 2x7=14
8+8=16 or 2x8=16
9+9=18 or 2x9=18
10+10=20 or 2x10=20
It's all the Same, but only Different.

> **It's all the Same, but only Different.**

10x10=100   or 10% of 100=10
10x100=1000   or 10% of 1000=100
10x1000=10,000   or 10% of 10,000=1000
10x10,000=100,000   or 10% of 100,000=10,000
10x100,000=1,000,000 one million dollars 10% of 1millon = 100,000
Lets look at multiples or multiple Tables

1	2	3	4	5	6	7	8	9	10
2	4	6	8	10	12	14	16	18	20
3	6	9	12	15	18	21	24	27	30
4	8	12	16	20	24	28	32	36	40
5	10	15	20	25	30	35	40	45	50
6	12	18	24	30	36	42	48	56	60
7	14	21	28	35	42	49	56	63	70
8	16	24	32	40	48	56	64	72	80
9	18	27	36	45	56	63	72	81	90
10	20	30	40	50	60	70	80	90	100

Chapter 5

Have you ever felt there was a super hero hidden inside you! When would you like to meet your super hero. It's time to let your hero out and you need to know where to look!

Very Important **Winning or loosing there is more to it? It's not just knowing How money works. That being very important. But you must have the proper Mind set! What does that mean? You see your Mind, Body and Soul must be completely with you in your growth and development. You can't have one more than the other. Or 2 of one and none of the other you must have all equally working together to be Successful.**

Some times people call Mind, Body and Soul referred to as Mental, Physical and Philosophical or Past, Present and Future All mean the same thing but only different. It's how it's represented and or what it represents in the current content. Lets put it Into terms that you can feel and see It's all about you and how you represent it, how you represent yourself. You see there are times to pull out the super hero in yourself

And let your super hero earn his or her keep as to say or pay there way. You and I know that your super hero can leap tall buildings and run faster than a locomotive and get things done that you and I alone fine difficult. Yet for them it's as easy as 1,2,3.

And they are successful at any thing. Yes, sometimes we get lucky and we win from time to time and have none these factors in order or in our life. But that is chance or luck! I like to increase my odds and change it to a sure thing that I can count on. You see it's like wanting something, but you don't know how to get it or where it is at. Or you don't know how to go about getting it. Think of it as you just need a map and instructions. And sure enough because you get the map the instructions and you follow them, Poof you get what you were looking for. But where is the map and instructions? Come on lets go find your super hero, your map and Key!

Would you like to meet your super hero?

You see most people run off going somewhere but don't know where they're going. Looking for things that are hidden right there in the safest of all places. Hidden in their own heart and soul hoping that you will come looking.

Let me give you an example: I tell you lets go and I'll see you there. You get in your car and tell me see you there. I leave excited to meet you there and when I get there you are no where around. You on the other hand got into your car and started out and realized that you didn't know where <u>there</u> was. You wanted to meet me there but where is there at? No matter how bad you wanted to be there or no matter how bad I wanted to share with you the joys and riches of being there. I could not and you would not be able to be there! No planning was made no directions or course was plotted. Make a plan it works!

No mater who your super hero is
or why, The true hero is YOU!
Be proud of that and you will always win
And you will get where your going.

Set a Course and you will get there!

A man by the name of Earl Nightingale once said, "if you are a captain of a ship and you set out to sea, and if you don't plot your course you would never reach your destination!" You would just drift aimlessly because you had no idea where you were going.

He also said: Don't drift your life away Make a Plan it Works!

Once there was a man that was cold and needed to build a fire for heat. He found a fireplace and put some wood into it, and told the fireplace give him heat. The fireplace said, I can't give you heat, not until you give me flame to burn the wood. Our lives we are like the fireplace, many times we want success or want to win but that alone is not enough. We want to be successful, but we are not doing what it takes to obtain our goal. Use the tools that are all around you, believe in yourself, but understand that alone may not always be enough. You may need do something to start the flame, take action get involved and truly believe in yourself. Some times to do that we need to believe in others until we have created our own flame.

They say "insanity" is doing the same thing over and over again and expecting a different result. Are you to stubborn to make the changes you need to win.

A man once had a safe and in it money and wealth. He would go to the safe with the key in hand, excited about his wealth and position it safely in the safe. But time in again and again he would return to his home broke and not a penny in hand failure over and over again! you see you are like that man, in your safe locked up safely in your Heart, Mind and Soul is success, your wealth, your happiness and joy. The only thing you need to do to access it, is put the key in and unlock your treasure. You may friend are the KEY. YMUM Note: I hope this book will help make many changes in your life. I hope it shows you how your life could be, with the understanding of Money. Try to use the strategies, concepts and your views of things you have learned. Now take them into your future relationships. Use a multitasking approach from now on, looking at things and expecting more from them be creative think out side the box.

Don't just read or play with your creativity. Let your mind take the examples, experiences and concepts of what is being said and take it to the next level. Based on your understanding, knowledge, examples, experience and creativity, the sky is the limit. Really enjoy the time you spend playing, talking, sharing, and reading this book. Now use it all to your advantage. Like anything in your life take the best out and throw the rest aside. I said throw it aside. Don't throw it away! Because you just may find that you can use other parts later on in life when it's time.

Now I am not getting all gummy and stuff but you need to know, what works today may not work tomorrow! And vise a versa as they say. So sometimes as we grow, we start to look at things a bit differently. Money also does that it changes as do markets, taxes, inflation not just sometimes but always! But, when you start making a bunch of money you have got to keep in mind where you came from.

The Natural Balance

- Don't sell yourself short and don't start to thinking you know it all. There's always more to learn. Always remember not only do laws change so do people and also the markets and the systems used. Always be open minded, and willing to look, think, and feel in a constant update.

- But the basics are for ever and keep yourself as part of the basics.

- Don't be afraid to Laugh, enjoy yourself, cry, hurt and express yourself but be real do it all in moderation. Work hard go fast and take it slow. Be patient first with yourself but don't baby and lie to yourself make things happen.

- Natural Balance

- You have got to break away the distance between your butt and the seat. Remember the difference between Winning and loosing is so small they touch. Don't be so close that you can't see the difference. Build a bigger margin.

- Keeping in mind that you need to be well rounded don't put all your eggs in one basket. But yet not so diversified that your lost. The balance think a little eastern culture Soft / Hard, Good / Bad, Equal / Opposite the Ying and Yang. The Ying & Yang the balance of power And it doesn't matter the kind or type of power. The balance is very important lets look.

Natural Balance

Think of it as the flow of Life…. Breathing.

Breathing in your nose out through your mouth. The chest raises and the blood gets more oxygen and the body gets feed from the food in the blood stream called circulation as your heart pumps the blood through out your body. You get stronger and your electrical system starts to send messages to the brain that it is ready and alive. This collaboration of all the functions of your body working together is a must for you to grow and stay in control.

In the East they believe that the body can heal it's self of Injuries and the Physical and Mental control of ones self is a normal natural thing. Well now for a second think of this in yourself. Your body is healthy, Happy and your having fun because your feeling good about yourself. Now you lookup and notice you are drawing people around you that are the same way Success Draws Success. And all of a sudden you relax and relaxation with in the effort your true expression develops.

You have just exercised yourself mentally and physically to being a success. And bigger than that, you found that you are able to share the most wonderful thing in the world YOU! You now believe in yourself and so do others. Just like learning to breath and then it become a natural function and you just do it. You can screw up and forget to breath or as you get older you don't mean to but at night older people just stop breathing. And they get sick and or have physical problems start to set in. Well Money works the same way, all of a sudden you stop watching it, stop working it, and it to falls apart. Try to stay on course and Make a Plan it Works.

What Direction are you Heading?

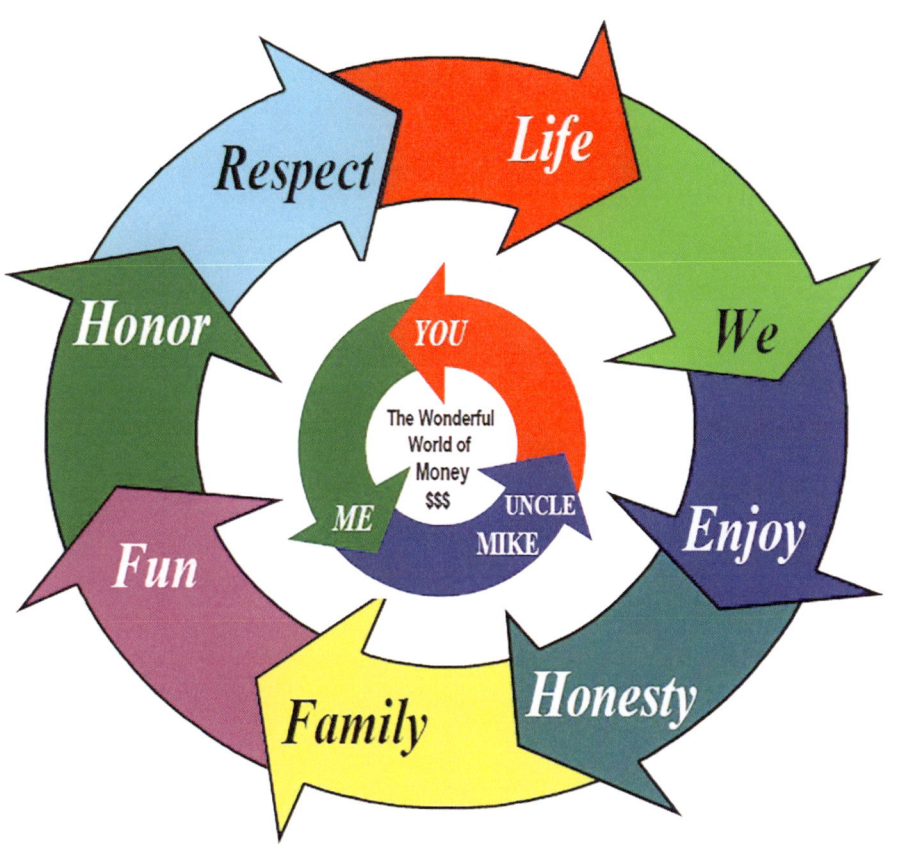

Simple Things

There was once a young fellow named Albert Einstein. He would tell people why would I keep every thing I know in my head, when I know where to find the information. If I need information go to the library where it is all gathered for me to use at any time. This way I can keep my mind clear and open for more important things. So I have prepared for you a short library for your review and future use.

Chapter 6

Simple Things like the graphs in this book are great, they will assist you though out your life. Some basic things never change. We understand that when we buy things we are paying for not only the item but for the various costs. The costs to assemble that item, the cost of shipping, packaging, taxes, and labor cost, warehousing, merchandising, fees, expenses and charges of different sorts. When we invest or have a checking account or anything like that we must account for our expenses so we know what our true return on our investment is called ROI, yield or net effective yield. That is the bottom line after all costs, expenses, taxes etc.

We will talk further about checkbooks, and/or passbook savings, mutual funds, stocks, bonds and more. We will learn how to combine strategies for the purpose of a better program for you to use to gain success. How to pick funds and the different charges, fees and expenses that you really need to know and how to use these items in you favor.

The secrets the wealthy use and why! It's called accountability when you are looking at things and seeing how you can make it better. When I go camping I always try to leave the place better than how I found it. My life is completed with that thought and that type of action. GIVE BACK ALWAYS, to know in your heart that you made things better than you found it, you are a quality person and that is Great! You my friend are Great it's time you let yourself and others know it...

A Penny saved is a penny Earned!

But think bigger than that, Save dollars!

Saving is a great and wonderful thing to learn to do. It may be saving rocks in your rock collection or bottle caps, cars anything that you consider of value. But, when saving money you get an additional bonus. You get more money due to interest!

Basically when you save money at a bank or credit union they will pay you an additional percentage rate of return on the amount of money you invest with them.

As an example the bank may pay you 2% to 3% interest on money that you put in their bank. Whereas a mutual fund could pay you 10% to 12% and then you have additional benefits as well.

There are certain things you need to do to win the money game. Like life it is all about strategies. You must learn to use the tools at hand and understand the job they do and don't do.

Bigger than that don't be afraid to learn to use things in a combination or work in collaborations together They can get more done, protect where one could not. Provide features and benefits that the others were not designed to do but together They compliment you and your goals. Lets look at the tools you will need.

Example Banks & Credit Unions: If you put $100 in a year later you would get $3.00 on your investment. So you would have $103.00 now this is where we really start to have some fun its called compound interest x 30 years later you would have $243.00 vs. simple interest of $90.00. Your money will start to double based on the rate of return. vs. e simple interest! Which like it says simple interest / gives you a percentage rate on your investment amount each and every time. Compound interest pays interest on interest it gives you a compounded rate or a doubling rate of return based on the interest rate.

Mutual Funds Example: the formula is if you get a 10% rate of return you just divide 10 into 72 and the answer will tell you how often your money will double every 7.02 years. What a great thing to learn, how to double your money and all you have to do is save it! Let's look at that again if you take the percentage rate of return divide it into the number 72 the answer is the amount of years it will take your money to double.

This is called compound interest. COMPOUND INTEREST

If you Invest $100.00 how many years will it take to double?

Rate of Interest/	years to formula	$100.00 Double	simple Total	1st year interest	30 yrs later Comp.	vs. Simple
3%	3 div into 72 =	24 years	$100.00	$3.00	$243.00 /	$90.00
4%	4 div into 72 =	18 years	$100.00	$4.00	$324.00 /	$120.00
6%	6 div into 72 =	12 years	$100.00	$6.00	$574.00 /	$180.00
8%	8 Div into 72 =	9 years	$100.00	$8.00	$1,006.00 /	$240.00
10%	10 div into 72 =	7.2 years	$100.00	$10.00	$1,745.00 /	$300.00
12%	12 div into 72 =	6 years	$100.00	$12.00	$2,996.00 /	$360.00
18%	18 div into 72 =	4 years	$100.00	$18.00	$14,337.00 /	$540.00

It's not just one thing that makes your money increase or decrease. It's making sure you do all you can to protect and let your money grow. You can reduce costs, fees, charges, taxes, and expenses count in inflation. Next you need to get the best rate of return on your investment! This is called getting the best yield. What that means is going through your investment and making all the adjustments you can To make it work harder, lower costs, reduce or eliminate taxes and basically keep more of your money. This is another form of Multi-Tasking doing more than one thing at a time and getting more than one thing done from each item and or its action or function.

Basically When you drive or walk down the street knowing where your going but you are enjoying the scenery along the way smelling the flowers and seeing the other people doing what they do and you are chewing bubble gum and reading the signs along the Way, yet you are still thinking about the job you will do when you reach your destination. With all this going on your maximizing the enjoyment the learning the efforts of all including things that you don't control like the sun and it's warmth or the cool breeze that make it nice. All in all your Growth and understanding is at it's best

Chapter 7: *Understanding Your Tools* and how to use them!

This is a section that most people make their mistakes. They simply don't use the tools available to them. I feel that once you have seen the pattern and the use of certain tools, you get excited with knowledge and can't wait to put these tools to work, use the right tools for the right job at the right time to be successfully. There are so many things in life that are necessary for us to make our lives work properly. Then there are some things that give us an advantage in our life to make our lives happier and more successful. We will cover the opportunities that most people never have had and or did not know were available. We will talk about the short cuts and extra things in life that make life easier. Note: We have a true challenge, sometimes people around us bring on negativity. Basically they are always looking at the short side of things. They will always tell you why things won't work or that you should not do it. But you know they don't have the education in that area or experience to give you true advice. Because they are your friend or family you have a tendency to believe them. Always remember people make mistakes they also have the people around them make mistakes and they are telling you that something doesn't work because of their mistakes.

You know your situation is not the same, every situation is different and unique so don't try to put a square peg in a round hole. Now what does that mean? Simple things don't work the same for everyone! Be smart take everyone's advice and or information and consider it all but keep what is good and throw aside the rest. Remember that times change, the information changes, and the world changes, what may not have worked a year ago may today. Remember that a person may have been doing it wrong or was advised wrong. There are some who don't want others to succeed where they have failed. Follow your own Path.

Mirror Mirror on the Wall

Reflections When you look in the mirror what do you see? Are you Really looking or are you embarrassed and quickly turn away. Or are you just interested I the Physical and fluff your hair and smile unconsciously. Or are you practicing the true Mind, Body and Soul look in the mirror and see the person you are, but understand the philosophy of the soul who, what and where you want to be. But yet you smile with confidence in yourself about how you mentally will continue your knowledge that gives you such a glow, such a physical shine and great health about you!

Now that's looking in the mirror. Mirror mirror on the wall who is the fairest of them all? Laugh and giggle and say me of course with your help!

When you look
In the mirror and
see yourself, are
you listening to
what you see, and
do you feel how
Wonderful it is to
be that person
in the Reflection.
Stand taller Next
time and taste the
pride and tickle of in
Your heart knowing
It's You and you're
Proud to be You!

Are you just looking at the reflections or are you really looking at you?

Do you have enough sense to get out of the Rain?

Sense to Common Sense

YMUM We will cover the common sense factor that a lot of people feel they don't have or some say certain people are born without. Of course I feel that once you see the pattern of common sense you will understand how you can have common sense in your life as well.

As an example: Do you have enough Sense to get out of the Rain. It's funny how some folks are not smart enough to do what is the natural thing, to do that becomes common sense. What does it mean "to have all your Ducks in a Row" It doesn't mean you should follow everyone in a line doing the same things the others are doing, just because they are doing it! No, it means get all of your affaires in order make sure you have all the things in your life working in the right direction for you! We will cover the joys and fun of different sayings and old phrases that for years have been said to us and why.

Yes it is important to lead and to be a leader, but sometime it is a must to learn how to follow! More people loose their fortunes and or lives because they never learn the Difference. When to lead and when to follow common sense teaches you that belief in yourself will allow you to be both leader and follower. You see leaders need to have support of there followers. Because a true leader will need you to take over and assist you in achieving your goals and dreams. Recognize who your leaders are in life, they are all around you! Lets take a trip and see who they are!

YMUM
The Right Road

Do You have an Idea
Where Your Going?

As we return Year after Year, We notice that there were many turns and paths along the way. Paths that you wished you would of, Could of, and even Should of gone down, but we passed up that opportunity or chance to successes and Win. We now understand we can control that Direction. It's our Road and Choices the directions we take and our success is a right of our Participation. And not a chance that you would walk by and miss any of your wonderful opportunities in life. Plan Your Road, Know Your Direction, Make it Happen take Control of Your life.

It's all about You!

Life's Roadmap and Directions

Enjoy your life, let yourself enjoy being you! Here you are ready to see the way it works? The secrets of success, the fun and the joys of life through learning, knowledge, common sense and thousands of years of what really works. They call it practical knowledge it helps you makes sense of things and use things in life now, before you get to old to enjoy it or loose the drive to do it. Don't forget to feel what you are going through. You are no longer afraid and you are aware of yourself and what your perimeters. The Joys of Success.

The roadmap to your life, with the confidence and ability to follow the map you make will make your dreams come true. If you truly believe! Finally you have reached that wonderful state, realizing you now believe in you! In Yourself! Most of the time people want to know things, but they don't know where to look or who to ask. The answers to these questions of course are right in front of you! Now we also have the web, which is a great tool right at your fingertips. Take advantage of this opportunity, stop wasting the another most valuable secret, Time. Time makes money you can't make more time you need to put more value on time and understand when you share your time with someone you have given them the most valuable gift ever.

This book as you can see from the title YOU, ME and UNCLE MIKE is involving Synonyms. We can have some fun with the same thing but only different concept. Things that sound the same or look the same even act the same but they are really totally different. It may be the same or nearly the same in meaning but written totally different. You see relationships with people or relationships with things or situations. Like the word "weather" or "whether" they sound the same, one is talking of the conditions outside rain, sun, or snow. The other is whether you aregoing or not, it means the difference of one thing to another, making a choice.

Life's Roadmap and Directions
are full of questions and answers. Sometimes the answer is the question.

You can see we can really have some fun with this in life, because so many things in life are the same but only different so the sooner we understand how to use these things the better results we can achieve for our own life's success. Frustration into insanity is doing the same thing over and over again and expecting a different result. What kind of results are you getting? Or are you even asking the right question or are you asking any questions are all. The important thing is are you asking yourself meaningful questions and truthful answering the questions? If you have noticed the key in most of this is the word yourself. It all starts there! And don't feel bad because you don't feel that you know the questions to ask most people don't the important thing is that you are listening. And if your let me teach you which questions to but bigger than that you are willing to answer the questions asked and if you don't know the answer like Albert Einstein we know where to go to find the answer. And yes as you are thinking knowing where to look is not the problem it is getting off your butt and expanding the distance from you and the chair and getting it done now.

Wonderful World of MONEY

We will cover the Wonderful World of MONEY, and how it can be a great thing for you and your family. Understanding money and how money works. I want you to be able to understand its use, calculation and the ability for you to control it for your benefit and that of your family. You will need and use money your entire life, it surely would be a great advantage if you understood it, and its perimeters. We will cover the art of counting and use of numbers along with strategies and the wonderful art of thinking and making agreements (GOALS) if you may. To make agreements that give you and others the opportunity to work together in a common goal that will benefit all concerned. Target what you want, what you wish, what you dream and make it happen.

This whole book is made and directed to show you how to make your life better, easier and more successful. Most people find out too late in life and never are able to use what they have learned. Laugh, giggle and have fun with your new found information and knowledge. Don't wait go for it, make it happen, You will find just by setting your mind to it you will start to succeed at every thing you do! You're new found awareness of yourself will open doors that were closed before. Don't hold yourself out, go for it! From here you will learn these secrets and short cuts in life, the building of usable knowledge that will make a great difference in your life and the success of reaching a happier more productive life. Set back and be patient and enjoy the fun of learning things that actually work and make life fun and worth while.

━━━━━━━

The bottom line is, you have got to have fun, make knowledge fun

Most of the time you hear of people saying where are they? Where are they am I going? What am I going to do? Who am I? Why am I here? Many people ask if some one could just show them how or give them a chance. They go through life waiting to find someone to show them the way. Most end up never doing any thing themselves, others get tired of waiting and just do it. Which will you be? Take control of your life. Truly Look at who you are and what you want to do, just do your best!

You must understand you are like a the universe a great empty mass of energy. You need to learn to Create. And fill this space of wonder, all you need to do is believe, believe in Yourself. Man is able to just by thought create from those mental images any thing he wishes. Fill the space with in create it in your mind and make it happen. Nothing can stop you but you, Dream and Believe and it will happen. Making money, being Successful, winning, helping others is all the same formula get up and go after It. If you think you can't, you won't, you have just stopped all growth just because you convinced yourself you couldn't do it. Think positive and your actions will be positive you will be positive you bring it on yourself. Notice that life is fun and happy when we just let it be! Participate with yourself If you go around being happy and fun. Notice that all the people around you Start to be fun and happy it's catching. Be the very best you can at everything you can. You were made with all the tools, knowledge and ability to succeed at any anything you wish. Reach out to the universe and give and take ask and feel for what you need and it will come. It's simple you will bring it on Yourself. Some say it's talking to God, some say it is energy to energy and Yet still others say it's some kind of law. Who cares Mikie says try it you'll like it . God says be the best person you can, use your abilities and make good use of who you are only by doing that can you help others.

A WIN, WIN POSITION

Like to Like if it can help you live a more complete and happy life. What do you have to loose, and everything to gain. Sharpen your skills reach out to the universe and grow be there for others because your there for yourself. Life is to short for you to be in doubt all the time, and before you know it's gone. Don't let life pass you Up! Most people do and they stand around saying I should of, I could of, I wish I would of but now they are to tired and to old and worn out to do anything about it. Or everyone is in a big hurry doing everything, and they get nothing done Bizzy bodies. Do you know anyone like that? So I ask you were are you going? And do you know where your going to be in 10 years from now? The big one do you know what you Want? From life, from your girl friend or boy friend, from your mom and Dad? If the answer is I don't know then what do you have to loose from learning how money works and how it can work for you. Just in Case you get a big idea and all of a sudden what or need to know how to get it. Or need the money to achieve it. Now your money ahead. You learned how to win how to learn how to believe in yourself.. You have taught yourself how to believe in someone else safely so you can learn and be a success yourself.

Chapter 8: Let's get back to the title YOU, ME and UNCLE MIKE

You see when I say words You or Me, you think of yourself as YOU. When you say the words YOU or Me, you think of me as YOU. You see, we just did it again. That's the whole point, it doesn't matter because all of the information you will learn is all about us. YOU, ME and UNCLE MIKE (US) the secrets of life works for all of us is the same way but only different because you are you and I am Me. But, even if we switch it around it means the same thing only different! (Success) because we both learned to use it together. If it will work for me it should work for you. You need to personalize things to your style and personality. But we all have the same right to Success, Honor, Wealth life it's not restricted to any one or anyone group.

YMUM as they say "What is good for the Goose, is good for the Gander." Now what does that mean? It means that if it's good for me it's probably good for you or if it is good for mom it is good for dad. Here we go again mom and dad or the male and the female same but only different. As mom is the wife or female parent and dad is the male parent, they both are mom and dad but now all of a sudden they are parents. When they come to school they become someone else, Mr. and Mrs. another form of the same thing, but only different. Back at home they become parents and parents don't seem to always see things the same way as you do. After you have just seen how they can change simply by name or title no wonder you are confused on what it is it that they want from you. Here's anothersubject we need to cover, what they want from you and what you want from them. The same thing, but only different. Maybe we can talk to them as equals or at least as mom and dad or as Mr. and Mrs. or by their first names. You just want to be able to talk openly with them. Let's be the Jones's and we unify as a family and that way we are all on even ground.

Family
This to me is so special and a true Honor.

Your family and your family name, one of the greatest things in life to share with the most wonderful people in your life! You will have this all your life, and with it comes Pride and Honor. So carry your father's name into the future and to give that name to your children. All the Great things that you and your children will do they will be remembered by your family name. A legacy I love that sound Legacy something that goes on and on, for ever and ever. Now what is the worth? Everything you can possibly make it, because it's truly yours IT'S YOU WHO YOU ARE.

I have met a few people that were not happy with their name or their father and mother. This is truly sad because they were abandoned by their father and mother. I told them Honor Thy Name, and make it special and give respect to your mother and father even if they do not deserve it because what you are doing is giving yourself respect and you need to have respect for yourself. Bigger than that is your Honor and there is nothing more important than that. Because my friend, it is yourself that you are honoring. When you and those around you, Honor you, then you are truly a success. If you don't respect yourself, then no one else can give you Respect and Honor.

Someone along the way has to establish the name, the pride, the respect, the honor, and make it special, what you are and what you will be! Why not you? Nothing is free! But there is nothing in the world stronger, more powerful more respected than your Honor. Smile and let that little grin and tickle in your heart enjoy! One day you will be the father or mother and you then will know what I say is true and will be glad that you taught your children to Honor to respect themselves in turn they will honor you with their endless respect.

- Family, mom and dad, brothers and sisters this is where we start our first encounter with agreements, negotiations, contracts, making deals with, understandings, rules and many other words that mean the same thing but only different called Respect. Remember the meaning changes depending on who says them. Just like the title YOU, ME & UNCLE MIKE changed whether you say it or I say it. So keep that in mind when talking to your parents make sure they understand the differences of when they say it and if you say the same thing. The Same, but only Different…

It's not what you say, but how you say It!

This will be our first opportunity to learn and practice the art of negotiations which is something you will need through out life. Your parents have been teaching you to negotiate since you were born from saying the magic words (Please) and (thank you), to If you clean your plate you will get something special! Remember your folks (your parents) same thing but different, they are in the middle of helping you get ready for life and that life is really a negotiation and the quicker you get at it, the better you will do in your life. 'Success," which is what they really want and so do you, is the goal!

Sometimes parents are not always looking at the big picture at your early age. So you must remind them that, what's good for the goose is good for the gander. Believe me you will gain respect and have fun with you folks, as well as probably get you what you want as well as they will get what they want. The same thing, but only different. Family and such a successful one.

Now it's your turn to take it to the next level, so what are you going to do with your new gained power and abilities.

To start sharing time with your parents to become An equal in the human race. To help them understand how to work together in a common goal. As always you will have to be the one to start the ball rolling but be patient With your folks and yourself. It's hard for them at first to see you are their Child that has now grown to the next level and they are slow at letting go of their baby. And yes you will always be their baby and believe me as long as you live you want to always hold that position. Just remind them that they have got to help you learn and do what they have been teaching you all your Life to do. And that's grow up!

Common Goal

Now this is powerful, you need to take some notes on this one! So let's say your parents keep telling you to clean your room or study or get better grades. This is a simple thing that both you and your parents benefit from. If you suggest that you both work together and they paid you an allowance each week then you could save and buy a new CD or Bike whatever it is you may want. This way you could save up your allowance and learn to manage your own money. You would be honoring your parents request and taking pride in yourself. It's all the same thing, but only different .

Now because you are looking at it from two points-of-view, one reaching a common goal that everyone can benefit from everyone in several different ways. And two to start negotiating with your parents, you might try to begin with cleaning your room. Look at the possibilities and benefits for both of you, that could come from that. You need to measure the difference between doing this negotiation and not doing it. What is in it for you and what is in it for your parents? You see it must be a two-way road or collaboration if you may. In making a successful deal for anything, it must be a winning deal for both sides. The sooner you learn to negotiate and do a good job at it the sooner you will win. Understand that you will have to negotiate throughout your life it only makes sense to learn do it well! Let me show you some of the simple benefits just from this one example of you cleaning your room for an allowance/money. Number one You start building a respect from your parents that will help you from here on. Two, Your parents give you money and you can buy candy, bikes, toys, I/PODS etc. Three, You get paid for what you would have had to do any way! And much more. Just think of all the possibilities for negotiations that can come from here, now you can negotiate with your parents for all kinds of things.

Most of which you have to do anyway so you might as well make it easier for yourself and learn from it and make everything in Life, works better as well as makes your life and your parents lives easier. It starts an opportunity for you to keep making deals with dad and mom, who have been trying to teach you this your whole life. And grandparents and eventually your boss for a raise!

Are you leading Your Life, or is Your Life Leading You!

Once you learn to work with people and be objective and fair, the next step is to learn the art of making money on your money in the bank, credit unions or the mutual funds this is called interest. The fun thing is you will put money in your account to keep it safe until you need it, and there are all kinds of ways to accomplish this! Think about it, you can now ask your neighbors if you can help them pick up leaves or what ever they may need help with. They will be so excited to have you asking them if you can help and of course it's good for you to earn some money! Now of course you can't and don't want to charge everyone for everything all of the time. Remember how we talked about "respect", well there are times like with your Grandpa & Grandma that you would honor them by offering to do things for free if they need your help. The fun part is that grandparents usually like to give you a little money anyway. They always want to encourage you to earn money and they will support your new working position.

Remember a lot of kids are messing up out there they are selling drugs, or stealing stuff and they are hurting people in their attempt to make money because they never learned how to negotiate or to honestly work together with their parents. They loose all the way around, they don't get anywhere they end up in jail or worse. And no one likes them and no one can trust them and no one wants them around. You see simply by learning to negotiate you win all the way around. You get better grades and the teachers are easier to work with and get along with! The other kids like you because you are a good kid and successful. Your parents are proud of you for doing your homework and for doing your work at home. You are learning because by doing your homework and doing well in school you learn all the things you will need to know to have a fun and wonderful life.

The secrets of life are like playing Mario or any of those computer games with a hidden door or star power or chest it give you that extra bonus of power to get to the next level. Well is much the same we have different times in life that we need to get that extra bonus the boost the simple helping hand or hidden secrets of life. Your teaches in your life are those hidden secrets that help you when your needing that extra boost. Don't forget to appreciate them and don't take them for granite. Now lets look at a simple example of how you could calculate it all and negotiate a winning deal for all concerned. Make it happen for you and others around you! You could agree to clean your room 7 days per week 52 weeks in a year. For instance if you could get your parents to agree on a $1.00 per day just for cleaning your room, it would be a place to start. We will call it an "allowance" not a payment or job, You see it's very important the words you use in a negotiation. If you charge $1.00 per day times 365 days a year that comes to $365.00 per year, man that is a lot of money! Only talk about it on a weekly or monthly basis.

It's not what you say, but how you say it!

Next, let your grandparents and aunts and uncles know that you are saving money in mutual fund for school and or things. Then ask them if they would when it comes to birthdays and othersuch things to please give you money for your mutual fund instead of any thing else, you have created another area in which to accumulate more money. You could also ask them if they needed some help that you would love to have the opportunity to help them. So you can earn more money for your account. Of course they all want to help you start this new saving plan so they start giving you money to see how and what you do with it and yourself. You see everyone around you wants you to succeed. It's not a question anymore of will you succeed but more like when. Make them proud, and let them help you be the best at everything you do, you gain respect for yourself and them and they do the same in return to you. Here's another area you could negotiate with your parents, maybe even your grandparents. Now the words you use and how you use them is so important! You would never say the words "pay you for" no, no it's a "reward" for doing something above and beyond. If you could get them to give you a certain amount of money for every A , B, or C and a bonus if you get more than one A a bonus if you don't get any tardies, for being late or detentions etc. They understand that you will be learning to save and it's your money hard earned that you are saving! Therefore you will value it much more because you earned it. This will show your parents that you are learning and doing quality things now and for your future. You are thinking on your own and need to be given the time, space and opportunity to grow. You see parents love to think they are directing their children in the right direction! They will be as proud of you as you are of yourself.

Negotiate Let's look at this again: You get a better grade that helps you now and in the future. Plus mom and dad is happy! You get the allowance to get the things you need or want. You're Happy! Your parents see that you are intelligent and are learning the basic skills of life. They are proud of you! Win, Win! Now you may have a stubborn parent from time to time but life will be the same way so you just as well start learning to deal with it! You may need to give them this book when you done reading it so they can be on the same page you are on... You are building working relationships with your parents. Trust, Respect and Honor! Your future opportunities are endless! You are building skills for a successful life! * Mom and Dad see you saving, getting better grades, they enjoy seeing you learn about value, and you and they are not yelling about what you want to do and what they want you do. They love having a relationship with you that is productive; it's for the success of both sides. Just so you know, your parents have been negotiating with you since you were born. They have negotiated everything from trying to get you to wash your hands, to eat, to smile, to taking medicine. They never looked at it to see and understand that it's the same concept but only different.

Thanks and Appreciation Parents really like it when they see their children showing appreciation and thanks for things. This is very important, you need to always show that you are respectful and appreciative to all the things people do for you. Remember to smile, be on the happy side, make your life enjoyable make your day and others wonderful and fun, enjoy and celebrate life. Appreciate your life and your family and friends, So many people forget that everyone does not have it as nice as you, So appreciation is key.

Chapter 9

Time is Money

Yes, money is important, but the most valuable thing there is in life is your TIME. So do special things, go visit your grandparents, spend some time with them. Ask yourself how valuable is your Time? 1 minute X 60 minuets = 1 * 1 hour X 24 hours = 1 day * 1 Day X 365 days = 1 year TIME is MONEY! The Time Value of Money is to understand that money grows based on time. Compound Interest is based on the rule of 72 where money doubles by the rate of return if you take the interest rate and divide it into the number 72 . The answer tells you how often your money will double. TIME VALUE OF MONEY is if you consistently invest year after year the value over time makes you the greatest gain. It's the amount of time you let it grow as it doubles. Another Factor is TIME: It's not TIMING of the Market, it's TIME in the Market! This is a very important thing to remember when making Money.

You have now learned the first steps of life, and that is to work things out for both sides. Now let's talk about that MONEY you earned. This is what the book is about, to teach everyone of all ages how to understand MONEY, which is a very valuable thing, this concept will help you succeed in life. I always think of myself as a child of knowledge, and a student of life. I never want to stop learning, or to think I have grown up, and out of learning. It's my hope you will feel the same way. Learning:

We must have a firm understanding of certain things in life. One of those is he word learning. The magic of learning comes from you. You see in order to learn some thing from some one or thing you must have trust. The trust in yourself, to take a chance and believe in someone or thing long enough for you to l earn it or something from them.

MAGIC ! When you were born you were born with natural knowledge. You were born with knowledge, your internal computer as to say, it's like magic it has automatically connected you to the big computer in the universe. It's a natural connection to knowledge; you just have to learn it! You just have to uncover it from within your mind. You have to have enough trust in you to believe in yourself to find out the information and put it to work. Now that's magic! You know it is really weird that that some people choose not to use there MAGIC. I mean everyone has it but some choose not to use it and they fight with themselves the rest of their lives trying to just survive. They basically hurt themselves and their families for the rest of their lives just because they refuse to believe in themselves. Now that's truly sad! Because you do believe in yourself, you can uncover all of this wonderful knowledge of the universe.

You, I and our families we can learn so much and then develop that knowledge and take it to the next level. When you were a baby you learned everything from your parents. You watch and learned, you trusted them enough to learn it yourself and then you did those things even better. You took what you learned to the next level. Continue to learn from others, believe in yourself so you can believe in others. They will teach you what you want to uncover. It's like common sense it's just there! If you use it or not is up to you! YOU SIPMPLY HAVE TO BELIEVE IN YOURSELF! Believe in yourself Sometimes we learn so much and develop it so far we take it to the next level, that we become the teacher. We become the one that actually knows more than the one that taught us. That's ok, it is called progress. This is so important you can never, I say again never, loose faith in these people. Just because you know more than they do in certain things, don't close the door.

The Many faces of Time

- The most wonderful thing of all things, the greatest gift of all, the most valuable thing that you now have learned is respect. RESPECT my friend to understand

- YMUM The biggest secret of all time RESPECT. Learning is wonderful but only as wonderful as you make it! You must give it value. Your parents were your first teachers, next are you school teachers, they deserve the same value of respect as do your parents.

- Don't Be a fool…If by chance you have a parent that is not the best of example of a parent. They are still your parents and you should still respect them even if they have not done or been there for you. Why you say,

- It's simple, you respect them even though they don't deserve it so that some day they will hopefully realize it. If you don't respect them, you can never expect your children to respect you, because you are giving the wrong example. It's got to start some where! Children learn by example, and you never ever want that happen to you! That, my friend is called Honor you honor them as you would HONOR yourself. To have the magic, and power the true magic you must have Respect and Honor for yourself to learn. Humility

When we become a great student of learning and a great teacher of knowledge we become the person of Humility. Now you want to talk about real power the real control of / and in Life! Understand Humility my friends and make good use of it. Be a person that knows that he or she <u>never</u> wants to stop learning or loose a chance of learning from people of knowledge. There is always something that we don't know," never burn your bridges." Think about it!

If you were to think a person, that has been your teacher or has taught you anything or everything. And you now think you're smarter than they are and mistreat them. I would say you just burned your bridge. You just lost a valuable teacher; friend and you lost respect for yourself. Never do that because that person has been apart of you, your past, present and future. They may have had more to offer you but they were going to offer it in a future opportunity as they and you have grown to. Maybe you may want in the future to have them on your team to develop something wonderful in the future. Never become so full-of-yourself that you loose the ability to learner. Be cautious of being a know-it-all, remember to practice Respect, and Honor, they are all rolled up in one word Humility, have reverence and take it to that place that you and only you may go!

The Many faces in life, the happy, the sad, the confused and so many more There like days of the year each one of there own. And yes each one of your own, you own them as they are your expression. Our interpretation, your view of what is taking place in your life. How you respond to these face of expression or interpretation is like a reflex an immediate reaction to Who you are be aware of yourself!

Chapter 10

I would like to talk to you about Multi-Tasking. Have you ever heard someone say, "he can walk, talk and chew bubble gum all at the same time?" That would be multi-tasking, when someone is doing more than one thing at the same time.

You will need to learn to do this as well. While studying your mom might say, "Come and eat" and while you were writing you still understood in your mind that you need to bring it to a close and go eat. You were just multi-tasking.

People can keep a lot of things going at the same time in their lives and the more we take control of ourselves, the more we can coordinate many things at once. This will become an art as you become more proficient with multi-tasking. When you add it to your everyday life it gets really fun. You allow yourself to travel at light speed and never leave the room, and when we combine it to work with our money, wow! Now that's cooking....Just like compound interest it's like magic when you learn to Multi- task properly.

Your understanding of the world and how it works, as well as how you can participate in and with the world Multiplies compounds. Now apply this to all of life and enter the light speed of your personal performance.

Let's talk Money $

Now, Let's talk MONEY: there are so many ways to deal with MONEY.

Things of value, money is one of them. But first let's go way back in time to understand the concept of money and things of value. Back in time before money was invented people simply traded and bartered. A farmer would trade the rancher vegetables for meat. The butcher would trade the rancher his meat, and the butcher would trade the farmer for eggs and vegetables etc., they traded services for services, or product for services. As time went on people decoded we need to build a "currency" to make it easier for payment for services and products, and currency was created and has evolved to today's current method. Now we we're able to base that currency on:

Gold,   Silver   OIL   Diamonds

We then could trade with other countries things of Value. And now we had a basis of value the Gold, Silver, Oil and Diamonds that were used around the world. In the United States we started making our own money that was backed by the government with Gold, Silver, Diamonds and Oil as well as other commodities. I want you to remember the very beginning of the book. We spoke of the SAME THING, BUT ONLY DIFFERENT. Well here we go again. THE SAMETHING, BUT ONLY DIFFERENT is COIN and paper CURRENCY OF THE United States of American.

Chapter 11

Money / Currency $$$

CURRENCY OF THE United States of American.
PENNIES,

It takes 5 pennies to make a Nickel.

        10 pennies to make a Dine.
        25 pennies to make a Quarter.
        50 pennies to make a Fifty cent piece. / Or a half a dollar.
        100 pennies to make a Dollar.

NICKELS
It takes   2 nickels to make a Dime.
            5 nickels to make a Quarter
            10 nickels to make a Half Dollar or a Fifty cent piece.
            20 nickels make a Dollar.

DIMES
It takes   5 dimes to make a Half-Dollar /Fifty cent piece.
            10 dimes to make a Dollar

QUARTERS
It takes   2 quarters to make a Half-Dollar.
            4 quarters to make a Dollar.

HALF DOLLAR / FIFTY CENT PIECE
It takes   2 Half Dollars to make a Dollar

DOLLAR 1 Silver dollar coin to make a Dollar
It Takes   1 Gold dollar coin to make a Dollar.
            1 Susan B Anthony coins to make a Dollar.
            1 paper dollar make a Dollar.

US CURRENCY as you can see has many forms of US Currency; here are a few more examples. The present denominations of our currency in production are $1, $5, $10, $20, $50 and $100 bills. The purpose of the United States currency system is to serve the needs of the public and these denominations meet that goal. Our present currency in circulation satisfies the public at large, and the Bureau of Engraving and Printing (BEP) has no plans to change the denominations in use today.

United States Notes/Legal Tender Notes

United States Notes are also known as Legal Tender Notes because of the wording of the obligation. These notes are the 2nd earliest type and longest issued U.S. paper currency to date. The issuance of these notes stirred a great deal of Constitutional debate over the legality of notes backed only by the credit of the U.S. government. Small size United States Notes were issued in series during the years of 1928, 1953, 1963, and 1966 in denominations of $1, $2, $5 and $100, but not all denominations were issued for all series. All series were titled "United States Note" except for the series of 1869 which was titled "Treasury Note" and the series of 1862- 1863 which had no title on the note. The wording of the obligation carried on the reverse of the notes was changed several times during the entire issue. The first issue dated March 10, 1862 consisted of all denominations from $5 to $1,000.

The earlier notes in this series carry the following obligation: debt." The fourth issue consisted of series 1882 and was printed in denominations of $20, $50, $100, $500, $1,000, $5,000 and $10,000. The fifth issue consisted of series 1888 and was printed in denominations of $5000 and $10000.

Just try to get anything with out money, it makes life a lot easier, and if you understand it more you will never have to worry about getting it, keeping it or the use of it. I have tried to teach you how to make money double, how to keep more of it and all about interest (making money on your money). As an Example: Checkbooks, Banks, Mutual Funds, Stocks, Bonds, Savings, Compound Interest vs. Simple Interest and the different types of money, the use of contracts, agreements, notes and taxes. You have already learned some of the benefits of agreements now let's learn how to make more money on your money that you earn. Make A Plan It Works!

Your Local Bank

Banking, know our Banker build a relationship with your Banker. Understand the services the Bank can offer you. Understand the charges and expenses. Balance is when you balance your charges with deposits and services, costs and expenses to have an account with the bank. All Must be considered. There are tremendous advantages to having a good Bank and Banking relationships.

1. Bank accounts, Checking, Savings, Debit Cards, Credit Cards.

2. CD Certificate of Deposits, cashiers checks, notary services etc.

3. Mortgage Service, refinance, loans, title

4. Loans: Auto, Personal, Business, Safety deposit boxes.

5. Estate planning Trust, Family Limited Partnerships, etc

6. Business Accounts, sweep accounts, Inventory Financing, etc

7. Certified or cashiers checks, Money Transfers and Bill Pay.

8. Wonderful services See your Banker today!

Local Bank, Your Neighborhood Partner

Checking Accounts are the first thing you all will come in contact with. Banks offer checking accounts which are a wonderful opportunity to start making an accountability of your money. The bank gives you a book of checks (paper that you can write an IOU for money.) Banks charge you to use their services, be cautious and aware of the real facts and that is cost, fees and charges.

Banks & Credit Unions

Checking Accounts! We have a bad habit thinking it's free and we don't account for the many charges that we incur for the services we receive some are visible and some are hidden The point is that they are there. You can write a check to the person or business when you want to buy something and the bank will pay the business or another person's bank the money. Of course you must have the funds in your account to cover the amount of the check you have written. It's a form of a contract that you make with the bank. But realize it's not done for **free** just because you have money in your account. And just because you have check doesn't mean you have money. If you write a check for more than the amount you have in your account or they will bounce (not pay) your check. **Bouncing checks** = not having enough money in your account to cover the check that you wrote. If that happens, the bank will charge you a fee for the bounced check.

Some banks offer what is called **"overdraft protection"** if you have that benefit feature on your account, the bank will go ahead and pay the check you have written. Usually this is contingent on you registering a credit card with them so they can charge the overage to it. If you do not have this feature, it can become very costly to you, because they will charge you a fee for bouncing your check, and embarrassment of not having sufficient funds to cover your check. You need to understand that the most important thing to Understand the fees & charges each month. Keep track of how much you spend (how many checks you write) so at the end of each month you can balance your checking account. That is subtracting all the purchases (checks you've written) from your balance as well as the expenses and charges and make sure you balance. You also subtract the charges that the bank has charged you for the fees to doing business with them. Some banks charge you by the number of checks your write and the deposits made, and some won't charge a fee if you carry a certain balance over each month.

Credit Cards

Credit Cards are also handled by the banks as well as other places. These are a plastic card that you can charge purchases, travel, buying items all around the world, food at restaurants or stores etc. Each card comes with what is called "credit line", which means you can charge only to that amount. These are very risky because of they charge interest on what you have charged if you don't pay it in full each month. Be very cautious with these! Banks offer all kinds of opportunities, Debit Cards a bit safer you only can spend the money in your account Like savings accounts, checking accounts, and loans. Some banks also sell mutual funds, stocks and bonds, most of the banks will write mortgage loans for people to buy their homes. The fun part of having a bank is that they are usually located in your neighborhood so it is very convent. Watch out for the 0% offers to transfer your old accounts to another. You must understand that when they transfer the new money from the old account to the new one. All of the money that was in the account you are transferring into has to be frozen and is not paid off until you get the new money at the 0% paid in full. Then they will start paying on the original debt. That means you are paying a higher interest rate on your original amount. Be extremely careful with credit card always pay them off each month. YMUM

"Can't see the forest for the trees" You're so involved you just can't see things around You.

"Money doesn't grow on trees" Don't be Wasteful, keep on Track, Value & Appreciation.

"A penny saved is a penny earned" We try to save! And if You do so, you earned it.

"The early bird catches the worm" Don't wait get right to it, the first one there Wins.

"First come first served" in a big family you learn to get to the table first or you miss out!

"Two for a Nickel " This is like multi-tasking, things do more than one thing at a time.

"Your two cents worth" This phase is giving your option even if no really cares.

"Bet you a dime to a dollar" when you are really sure your right! Don't forget who you are and where you come from and be proud of where you been!

It's simple everyone needs a Professional once in awhile. When it is so Important to get the job done right! Your Future happiness and family financial security depends on it. YMUM will show how to achieve your goals and dreams! Share this information with those you care for family, friends, co-workers.

Let your money work harder, while you work smarter

* Ywour 401k & IRA Rollovers.
* Learn the Secrets the Wealthy Use.
* Set-up and Create Income for Life.
* Tax Free benefits of the ROTH-IRA.
* Create a Tax Free Retirement Income.

We teach you how to maximize your financial future through financial education.

You, Me & Uncle Mike

Chapter 12

WINNING THE MONEY GAME

1. **SAVE MONEY** on A Regular basis.
2. **WIN** the Rate of Return Battle.
3. **WIN** the Tax Battle

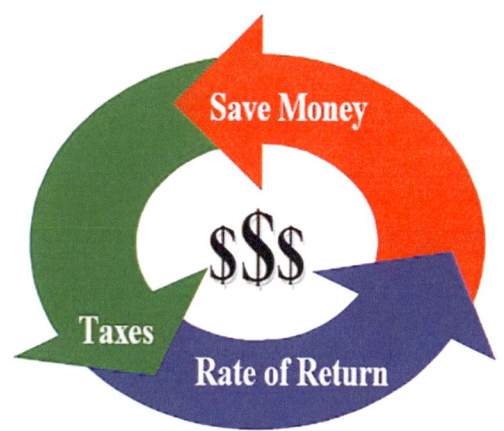

"With Money you can buy" a House but not a Home!

"With Money you can buy" a Clock but not Time!

"With Money you can buy" a Bed but not Sleep!

"With Money you can buy" a Book but not Knowledge!

"With Money you can buy" a Doctor but not Health!   74

"With Money you can buy" a Position but not Respect!

"With Money you can buy" a Blood but not Life!

INFLATION

- ## Inflation 3% to 4% over the past 20 years.
The cost of Money Increases Daily!

Average Home 20 years ago $24,910 * Average Home Today $150,000

Inflation Vs. Income

Today's $	$30,000	$40,000	$50,000	$60,000	$100,000
10 years	$48,867	$65,156	$81,455	$97,734	$130,312
15 years	$62,368	$83,157	$103,920	$124,736	$207,840
20 years	$79,599	$106,132	$132,665	$159,198	$236,330
25 years	$101,591	$135,454	$169,318	$203,112	$338,636
30 years	$129,658	$172.878	$216,097	$259,316	$432,194
35 years	$165,480	$220,641	$275,801	$330,960	$551,602
40 years	$211,200	$281,600	$351,999	$422,400	$703,998

Time Value of Money * Don't Procrastinate

Does 1% Make a Big Difference?

The Future Value of $200.00 Per Month
Invested at Various Interest Rates

% Rate	10 Years	15 Years	20 Years	25 Years	30Years
6%	32,775	58,100	92,400	138,000	201,000
7%	34,000	63,300	104,000	162,000	243,000
8%	36,000	69,200	117,000	190,200	298,000
9%	38,000	75,600	133,000	224,200	366,000
10%	41,000	82,900	151,000	265,300	452,000
11%	43,000	90,900	173,000	315,200	560,000
12%	46,000	99,900	197,000	375,700	699,000
13%	49,000	109,900	226,000	449,400	874,000
14%	52,000	121,100	260,000	539,100	1,098,000
15%	55,000	133,700	299,000	648,700	1,398,000
16%	58,500	147,700	345,000	782,600	1,750,000
17%	62,000	163,500	398,000	946,500	2,220,000
18%	66,000	181,000	461,000	1,147,400	2,822,000

Time Value Of Money $$$

COST OF WAITING

P r o c r a s t i n a t i o n

Age				
25	2,000	2,260	0	0
26	2,000	4,814	0	0
27	2,000	7,700	0	0
28	2,000	10,961	0	0
29	2,000	14,645	0	0
30	2,000	18,809	2,000	2,260
31	0	21,255	2,000	4,814
32	0	24,018	2,000	7,700
33	0	27,140	2,000	10,961
34	0	30,668	2,000	14,645
35	0	34,655	2,000	18,809
36	0	39,160	2,000	23,515
37	0	44,251	2,000	28,831
38	0	50,004	2,000	34,839
39	0	56,504	2,000	41,629
40	0	63,849	2,000	49,300
41	0	72,150	2,000	57,969
42	0	81,529	2,000	67,765
43	0	92,128	2,000	78,835
44	0	104,105	2,000	91,343
45	0	117,639	2,000	105,478
46	0	132,932	2,000	121,450
47	0	150,213	2,000	139,499
48	0	169,740	2,000	159,894
49	0	191,807	2,000	182,940
50	0	216,741	2,000	208,982
51	0	244,918	2,000	238,410
52	0	276,757	2,000	271,663
53	0	312,735	2,000	309,239
54	0	353,391	2,000	351,700
55	0	399,332	2,000	399,681
Total	12,000		52,000	
Earnings	$399,332.00		$399,681	
@ 65	$1,343,559.00		$1,326,373	

How Money Doubles Compound interest

Rule Of 72
How Money Grows Compound Interest

18 Yr 4%/72		12 YR 6%/72		6 YR 12%/72		4 YR 18%/72	
1	$10,000	1	$10,000	1	$10,000	1	$10,000
				6	20,000	4	20,000
						8	40,000
		12	20,000	14	40,000	12	80,000
				18	80,000	16	160,000
18	$20,000					20	320,000
		24	40,000	24	160,000	24	640,000
				30	320,000	28	1,280,000
						32	2,560,000
36	40,000	36	80,000	36	640,000	36	5,120,000

Compound Interest - How Your Money Doubles ! You simply take the interest rate and divide it into the number 72 and the answer will tell you how often your money Doubles

73

Let Your Money Work Harder, While You Work Smarter.

Professional Money Managed Accounts
MUTUAL FUNDS

A Mutual Fund is a Pool of Professionally Managed Money
averaged 12% return since 1924

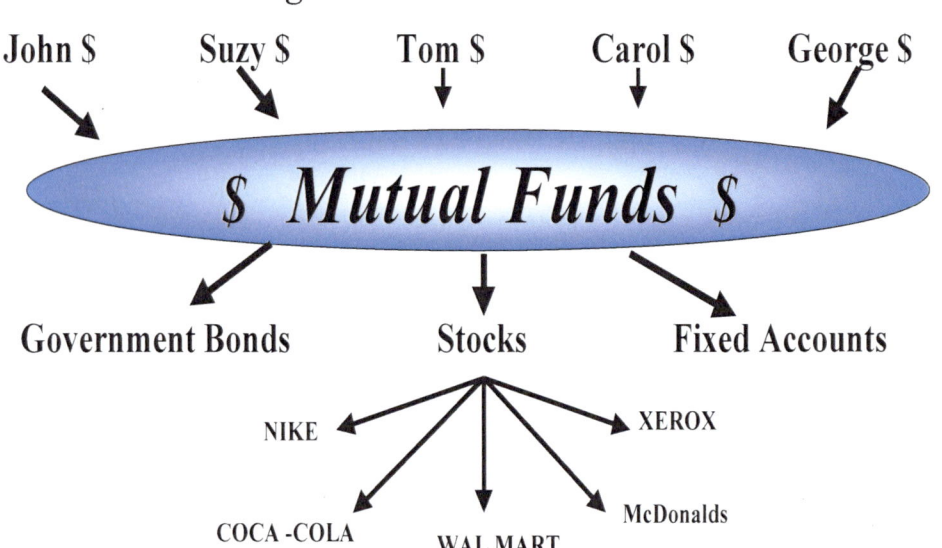

Tax Strategies * Keep more of your Money

Tax Strategies - There are 3 ways to Accumulate Money in America Today

 # Taxed
Pay as you Go!

 # Taxed Deferred.
401k, IRA, Annuities,Qualified Plans etc.

Tax Free.
Roth-IRA's, Insurance Accounts, Bonds etc.

It's up to You? It's Your Choice…
How do you want your Money to Grow?

Never Put all your eggs in one Basket!

Make A Plan That Works

TAXED	TAX DEFERRED	TAX FREE	TAX FREE NON-QUALIFIED
$1,000.00 28% Fed 7% State 35% Taxes $1,000.00 - 350.00 $650.00 $350.00 @ 12 %X 30 years $1,078,341	401k, 403b, IRA's SEP-IRA Annuities 59 1/2 Grows Tax Deferred 10% penalty Plus Tax	Roth-IRA's Bonds 59 1/2 Grows Tax Deferred 10% Penalty ?plus Tax	Variable Universal Life UL VUL Whole Life Tax Shelter $$$ $$$ 59 1/2 Grows Tax Deferred Withdraw Income Tax Free

Investment Task Baskets / Tax Baskets

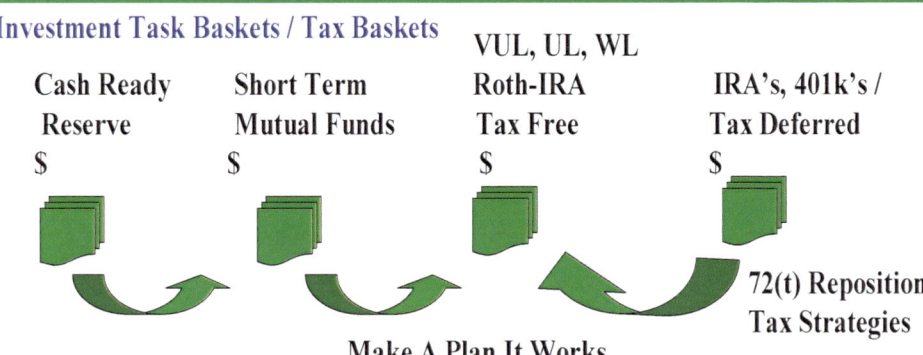

| Cash Ready
Reserve
$ | Short Term
Mutual Funds
$ | VUL, UL, WL
Roth-IRA
Tax Free
$ | IRA's, 401k's /
Tax Deferred
$ |

72(t) Reposition
Tax Strategies

Make A Plan It Works

Understanding Taxes & Inflation

You will need more than your thinking!

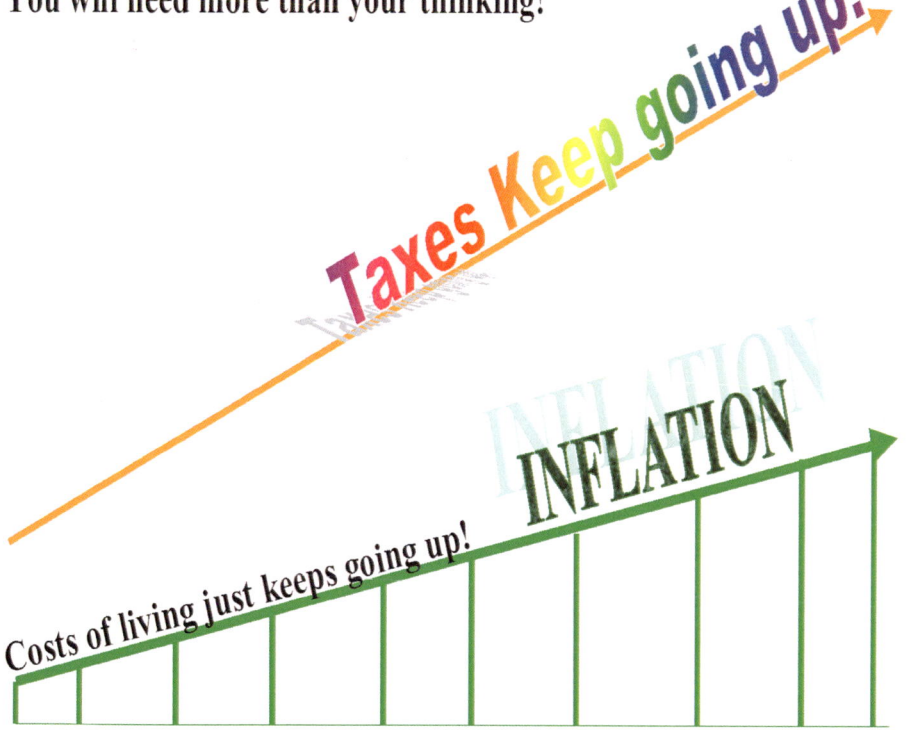

Chapter 13

PROCRASTINATION

**Don't keep putting it off get started today,
time makes money Compound Interest!**

$4,000 per year, 10% return[1]

Age	Bill 35 Years old	Tom 25 years old
25-34 (10 years)	$0 per year	$4,000 per year
35-44 (10 years)	$4,000 per year	$0 per year
Amount invested	$40,000	$40,000
Value at age 45	$72,037	$195,006
Value at 65	$527,889	$1,429,017

I wish I would of !
I could of !
I should of !

Don't WAIT!
Just Do It !
Start NOW !!!

Who's Really First ?

WHAT BILLS DO YOU PAY FIRST?

YOU!!! And Save

Mortgage Payment

Cell Phone Bill

Car Payment

Cable and Satellite

Food

Water Bill

Computer Payment

Vacations

Light Bill

YOU NEED TO SAVE AT LEAST 15% OF YOUR INCOME

Let Your Money Work for You!

Are You Working Hard for Your Money?

or

Is your Money working hard for you?

Work Smarter not Harder!

Understanding what Makes the World go Round

Money make the world go round make sure your money is working for you and let your money work Harder while you work smarter!

Investments in people, companies, stock markets, Art, Property, Precious metals, so many different Items at your choice Be smart let your Money work for you!

Invest

You Me and Uncle Mike
What Direction are you Heading?

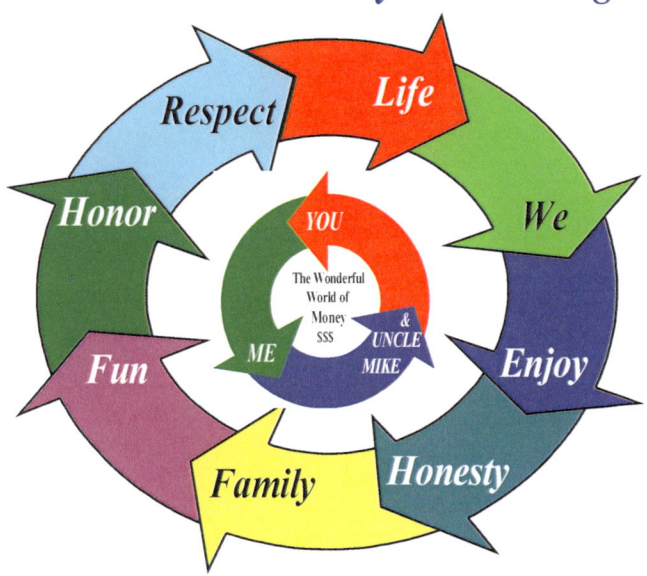

You Me and Uncle Mike
A Book for Kids of All Ages
The Same Thing But only Different

Exercise your (Multi-Task) skills Order your New Financial Education Series of Book and Disc's available at all participating Stores.

Read them all, read them together. Look at ever thing from different points of view to making your personal Strategies. And then take them to the next level. The Secret is to be patient with yourself and others, have fun it works Better and Faster that way!

Your Friend always Uncle Mike

Who's Hat are you wearing today!
The Aggressive Investor,
The Moderate Investor,
The Cautious Investor,
The Passive Investor,
The Foolish Investor,
The Scared Investor,
The Happy Investor,
The Wise Investor,
The Sad Investor

Be an Educated Investor

Watch for all the New Uncle Mike's Financial Education Series of Books coming to You!

You have completed the first book of You, Me and Uncle Mike. There are many things that you have to ask yourself? Take a look at all the things that we have covered and use them in relationship to each other. (Multi-Task) them all together. Look at ever thing from different points of view. Note that everything can be applied to anything and everything in Life. Now take them to the next level. The Secret be patient with yourself and others, it works Better and faster!

Your Friend always Uncle Mike

Chapter 14

Strategies and Basics

1. Principals that you need to incorporate.
- **Understand your objective.** What is it your trying to achieve.?
- **Develop a Financial Plan.** Write out your plan!
- **Set long Term Goals.** If you don't set goals how will you get there.
- **Build a Allocation strategy.** How do you want your money to grow
- **Always Review You Plan.** Hold people and companies accountable
- **Harness Taxation,** understand Taxed, Tax Deferred, Tax Free!
- **Market Shifts and Changes** Emotions out, Concepts & Strategies
- **Marketing Timing** It's not timing of the market, It's time in the market
- **Dollar Cost Averaging** The daily values all average out! don't be impatient.
- **Keeping Track** Make a Plan It works, Now follow It! Time is Money!
- **Stay Fast** Don't be jumping around every year let it work.
- **Your Legacy** Keep in mind family protection, and an exit strategies.
- **Procrastination** don't wait, I should of, would of, could of, get it done

MONEY

Each and every year we face the Road of Life!

If we take the same road year after year we will always end up in the same place. In January of each year we look down that road. We always make New Year's resolutions, things like to lose weight, make more money, exercise or to make some kind of changes in life.

We go down that road year after year from January to December. Hoping to find the Path or turn that leads us to our secrets. The Secret path that leads us to Happiness, Success, Love, Joy, Knowledge, Riches, and Peace.

As we return Year after Year, We notice that There were many turns and paths along the way. Paths that you wished you would of, could of, and even should have gone down, but we passed up that opportunity, that chance of successes and winning.

We now understand we can control our direction. It's our road and our choices the directions we take. Our success is a right of our participation, and not just chance. Don't take the chance that you would walk by and miss any of your wonderful opportunities in life.

Plan your road, know your direction, take a helicopter view of your Road of life. Look down and see where it goes and where the turns are now you see, where you should of, could of, or will turn this time. Make it Happen take Control of Your life.

It's all about You!

Which Road
do I Take

Chapter 15

- **Accredited Investor:** An accredited investor is an officer within a company or someone who meets certain financial requirements. Issuers who have offerings that are exempt from formal registration must know an investor is accredited or non-accredited.
- **Accrued Interest:** The amount of interest the bond buyer owes to the seller. Because bond transactions do not usually occur on the exact day the issuer pays the seller the dollar amount of interest which has accumulated on the bond since the last interest date. In addition, the buyer pays the market value of the bond.
- **Accumulation:** The first phase of a bull market. Accumulation of shares while earnings are at their worst and the economy is declining.
- **Accumulation Unit:** The unit an investor receives during the accumulation period of a variable annuity. The dollar investment divided by the accumulation unit value equals the number of accumulation units acquired with each investment.
- **Affiliated Person:** A person (either natural or a corporation) who owns 5% or more of the outstanding voting securities in an investment company or any officer, director, partner or employee of such person. If the affiliated person is an investment company, the investment adviser is also affiliated. The Investment Company Act of 1940 defines and regulates affiliated persons.
- **Agent:** See broker
- **Aggressive Growth Funds:** Investment companies which have invested most of their portfolio assets in stock, generally in smaller corporations, that have the chance of increasing in value at a faster rate. Also called "small cap" funds.
- **Aggressive Growth Portfolio:** A diversified portfolio of common stock with high potential growth.
- **AIR:** An assumed interest rate (AIR) is used as a basis to compare with the actual investment return. If the actual return is greater than AIR, the annuity unite value will increase. AIR is used during the pay-out period of a variable annuity.
- **Alpha:** The premium a security earns above a set standard. Alpha is generally measured in terms of the S&P 500 Index. A measure of how a security performs independently at the market.
- **Amortization:** The straight-line deduction of capital expenses such as certain business startup costs and construction period interest, etc., over a fixed period (generally a shorter period than the rest of the property). For example, a $10,000 expense amortized over 10 years is deductible at the rate of $1,000 per year.
- **Annualized rate of return:** The average return over a period of years, taking into account the effect of compounding. Also known as the compound growth rate. For example, a 1005 return over five years is equivalent to an annualized rate of return of 18.2% per year.
- **Annuitant:** A person who receives income from an annuity.
- **Annuity:** A written contract between an insurance company and a contract owner. The owner pays premiums to the insurance company and in return the company later pays income to the annuitant.
- **Annuity Unit:** An accounting measure used during the pay-out period of a variable annuity. Once the annuity is annualized (payments begin to the annuitant), the number of annuity unites times the value of each unit determines the annuitant's payment.

Vocabulary

- **Appraisals (evaluations):** An appraisal is done on bonds that are infrequently traded to determine a market value. By comparing similar issues of bonds that have recently traded, a price estimate can be made based on the bond's coupon, maturity and quality.
- **Appreciation:** An increase in the value of a security.
- **Asked Price (Offering Price):** For mutual funds, it's the price at which a fund will sell shares to the public. For an OTC security, it's the price at which one dealer will sell to another dealer.
- **Asset:** Something of worth owned by an individual or corporation. For example, property, equipment and securities.
- **Average Price:** A simple averaging computation that divides the total purchase price by the total number of purchases or shares owned.
- **Back-end Load:** A fee charged by some mutual funds when shareholders sell shares back to the fund.
- **Balance Sheet:** A financial document that shows the net worth of an individual or corporation. For an individual, the computation is: total assets minus total liabilities equals net worth. For a corporation, the computation is total assets minus total liabilities equals stockholders' equity.
- **Balanced Fund:** A fund that seeks both growth and income, with stability of principal, through a portfolio that includes both stocks and bonds.
- **Basis:** The basis is usually the cost of an asset with any appropriate adjustments. For direct participation programs the basis of the asset determines the amount of deductions.
- **Basis Point:** A bond basis point is 1/100th of a percentage point. Shown as a percent it's .01%, as a decimal it's .001. In other words, one percent of a bond is $10: therefore, 1/100th of $10 is 10 cents. One basis point is equal to 10 cents.
- **Bear Market:** A prolonged decrease in the securities market.
- **Beneficiary:** A recipient of proceeds from a qualified retirement or insurance policy upon the death of the registered owner.
- **Beta:** A measurement of a stock's risk or portfolio's risk in relationship to the market as a whole. High beta stocks perform well during a bullish market and are sluggish during a bearish market.
- **Bid Price:** For mutual funds, it's the price at which a customer can redeem shares. The bid price is also called the NAV (net asset value). For OTC security, it's the price at which one dealer will buy from another dealer.
- **Blue Chip Stock:** in seasoned companies, large in size with a good dividend track record.
- **Blue Sky Laws:** Another name for state securities laws. The nickname occurred because states passed laws to protect investors and to enforce penalties when agents sold a piece of the "blue sky" to investors (promising specific returns, unrealistic expectations or misrepresenting the security).
- **Board of Governors:** The controlling body of NASD board selected by a committee.
- **Bond:** A promissory note (debt security) by a government or corporation to raise capital.
- **Bond and Preferred Stock Funds:** An investment company that invest its assets in bonds and preferred stocks. These funds are designed to generate income.

Vocabulary

- **Bond Fund:** A mutual fund that invest most of its assets in bonds. The objective is preservation of capital with steady income.
- **Bond Rating:** A rating for a bond by an independent rating service such as Standard & Poor's Corporation, Moody's Investor's Service or Fitch. These ratings are assigned based on the issuer's ability to pay interest and principal as agreed. Ratings range from "AAA", the highest, to C's or D's the lowest.
- **Book Value:** The net worth, or liquidating value of a business. Calculated by subtracting from total assets all liabilities, including debt and preferred stocks, and dividing by bye number of shares of common stock outstanding.
- **Break-even Point:** With an option contract, the market price at which the underlying security must move so the investor doesn't lose any money. He/she simply breaks-even.
- **Breakpoint:** A schedule of reduced sales charges for lump sum or cumulative purchases over a set time period in a mutual fund or variable annuity.
- **Broker (Agent):** A licensed or registered person who buys and sell securities for a customer. The broker acts as an agent by bringing the buyer and seller together and charging a commission. The amount of commission is disclosed to the customer. This is an agency transaction.
- **Broker/Dealer (B/D or Brokerage Firm):** A securities firm that acts as a broker or dealer on a particular transaction.
- **Broker's Broker:** A broker that brings together municipal securities brokers and dealers and charges a commission (agency transaction). Also, a specialist who brokers orders for a commission house broker.
- **Bullish:** Generally a longer period of time in which prices rise.
- **Bull Market:** a prolonged increase in the securities market.
- **Buying Power:** The amount of securities that can be purchased with the Reg T excess in a margin account Capital Appreciation: An increase in the value of a security or asset, such a mutual fund shares. Capital appreciation is the investment objective of mutual by fluctuating employment levels, industrial productivity, and interest rates.
- **Capital Gain Distribution:** A payment to mutual fund shareholders of profits (long-term gains) realized on the sale of securities owned by a mutual fund. The net asset value of the fund is reduced by the amount of the capital gain distribution, and additional shares issued to the owner.
- **Capital Gain (Loss):** A profit (selling price minus cost basis) or loss on the sale of a stock, bond or other asset. Short-term capital gains refer to a gain on assets held for one year or less. Long-term capital gains refer to gains on assets owned for more than one year.
- **Capital Stock:** The number of shares and total par value of an issuer's outstanding common stock and preferred stock are shown under "capital stock" on the issuer's balance sheet.
- **Capitalization:** The amount of capital from equity (common and preferred stock) and/or long- term debt securities and retained earnings.
- **Capitalized:** An expense which is deducted over a period of time 9capitalized) rather than being deducted as a current business expense.

- **Cash Account (Special Cash Account):** A customer's account at the broker/dealer where payment is made in cash or with a check.
- **Cash Accounting:** An accounting method used to determine the income and expenses of a company. Income is accounted for when it's received. Expenses are accounted for when they are paid.
- **Cash Flow:** The cash inflow to a company minus its cash outflow equals its net cash flow for a specific time period. Cash flow can also be analyzed for a specific investment.
- **Cash Trade (Cash Delivery/Cash Transaction):** The seller delivers the securities and the buyer pays for them on the same trade date.
- **CD (Certificate of Deposit):** Certificates issued by commercial banks in exchange for a deposit. The certificate holder receives interest and the deposit at maturity.
- **Certificate:** A certificate which verifies either ownership or a creditor of the issuer. The certificate includes the name of the issuer, number of shares, face value for debt securities and the name of the owner. Often times the back side of the certificate will include other pertinent information to the issue and a fill in the blank section to transfer ownership.
- **Certificate of Incorporation:** A formal certificate issued by a state which recognizes a business as a corporation.
- **Certificate of Limited Partnership:** A certificate that's filed with a state to organize a limited partnership. The certificate contains information concerning the nature of the partnership's business including a list of general and limited partner, amount of contributions and other pertinent information.
- **Churning:** Excessive trading activity in a customer's account induced by a registered representative to generate commissions instead of meeting the customer's objectives. This practice is prohibited.
- **Class:** All options of the same type (puts or calls) on the same underlying security.
- **Closed-end Fund:** A regulated investment company that offers a fixed number of hares, which are traded on a stock exchange, and can be traded in the same manner as stocks.
- **Closed-end Management Company /Publicly Traded Shares:** An investment company that issues a limited number of shares and manages the assets in its portfolio. An investor owns shares in the investment company and the company owns the shares in its portfolio. The portfolio is invested in the stock market. The company will not redeem its shares; they are sold in the open market. The price is determined by supply and demand for the shares in the open market.
- **Collaboration** working together, to unite, a common Goal.
- **Collateral:** Securities or assets pledged by a customer to a bank or broker/ dealer to obtain a loan.
- **Commission:** The compensation a registered representative or broker receives for executing a customer's order.
- **Common Stock:** A security which is convertible into another. It generally describes convertible preferred stock and convertible bonds. The security has a specific conversion rate at which the security can be converted.
- **Compounding:** Interest paid on interest, resulting in an exponential rate of increase on the initial principal. For example, an investment yielding 5% compounding annually, a $1000 investment would be worth $1050 at the end of one year, and then would generate 5% of $1050 in the second year and so on.

- **Consumer Price Index:** The change in consumer prices determined monthly by the U.S. Bureau of Labor Statistics, often cited as a general measure of inflation.
- **Convertible Bond:** A bond that the holder has right to convert to common stock of issuer.
- **Convertible Security:** A security which is convertible into another. It generally describes convertible preferred stock and convertible bonds. The security has a specific conversion rate at which the security can be converted.
- **Corporation:** A legal entity organized according to the laws of the state in which it incorporates. It separates the officers' personal assets from the corporate assets. The corporation is owned by the investors who own its outstanding common stock. The corporation has unlimited liability. The stockholders have limited liability.
- **Cost Basis:** For determining depreciation, it's the original price or cost (purchase price) of an asset. For determining a gain or loss on a security transaction, it's the portion of the investment on which the investor has already paid taxes.
- **Coupon Bond (Bearer Bond):** A bond that has coupons attached to the certificate which the bondholder must send to the issuing corporation's trustee when interest payments are due. At maturity, certificate is sent to the trustee and the principal is returned to the investor.
- **Coupon Rating:** An evaluation of the creditworthiness of a debt security by an independent rating service.
- **Covenants:** Promises in the bond contract which require the issuer to protect the interest of the bondholders. issuer must keep the property insured in case of fire insurance covenant.
- **CRAT:** Charitable remainder annuity trust.
- **Credit Balance (CR):** The credit balance includes the client's margin amount and the proceeds h/she received by selling the securities short. This credit balance is actual cash and it serves as collateral until the stock loan is repaid.
- **Credit Risk:** The potential for default by an issuer on its obligation to pay interest or principal on debt securities. The lower the rating of the issue, the higher the interest rate the issuer must pay to attract investors.
- **CRUT:** Charitable Reminder Unit Trust
- **Cumulative Preferred Stock:** A preferred stock which accumulates dividends that are not paid for possible future payment. Dividends in arrears must be paid to cumulative preferred stockholders before anything is paid to common stockholders.
- **Current Assets:** Assets that are convertible into cash within one year. Examples include: cash, marketable securities, short-term investments, accounts receivables, notes receivables, inventory and prepaid expenses.
- **Current Liabilities:** Liabilities that are due and payable within one year. Examples include: accounts payable, accrued expenses payable, interest payable, notes payable and income taxes payable.
- **Current Yield:** The yield and investor currently receives upon purchase of a security. The annual dividend or interest divided by the purchase price of the security equals current yield.
- **Custodian:** A person who's responsible for protecting the assets individuals or corporation.
- **Date of Record:** The date established by a corporation to determine which shareholders are on record to receive at the upcoming dividends.

- **Day Order:** An order which is good until the close of trading on that day. Orders are assumed day orders unless indicated otherwise.
- **Debit Balance (DR):** The amount of money the customer has borrowed from the broker/dealer to buy securities on credit. The debit balance is an open-end collateralized loan since the stock serves as collateral no pay off date or monthly installments on the loan.
- **Debt Securities:** General term for any security representing money loaned that must be repaid to the lender at a future date. Bonds, notes, bills, and money market instruments are all debt securities.
- **Deferred Annuity:** An annuity that defers income payments until some future date.
- **Defined Benefit Plan:** The corporation defines the fixed benefit that each employee will receive at retirement. The actual amount the corporation contributes to the plan is determined by actuarial assumptions.
- **Defined Contribution Plan:** The corporation defines the fixed contribution that will be made into each eligible employee's account. The actual benefit the employee receives at retirement depends upon the length of time the employee is covered under the plan, the amount contributed by the corporation, the expenses and the plan's profits.
- **Depreciation:** A deduction against the property's income which allows an investor to recover the property cost. The yearly depreciation deduction is certain percentage of the property and is taken over a set number of years. The property must be used for business or the production of income, have a determinable life of more than one year and wear out, become obsolete or lose value due to natural causes.
- **Derivatives:** A security that derives its value from anothersecurity. For example, the value of an option is tied to the value of the underlying security the option is written on. The value of mortgage pass-through securities is tied directly to the value of the mortgages Dilution: A decrease in the existing shareholders' equity position in the company since some or all of the issue's convertible securities were converted. When convertible securities are converted to common stock, it dilutes the existing shareholders' percent of ownership Discount Rate: interest rate charged member banks to borrow money from district bank.
- **Discretionary Income:** income an investor has left after necessary expenses are paid.
- **Distribution:** Payment of a dividend or capital gain by an open ended mutual fund. May be taken in cash or reinvested in additional shares of the fund. The condition in which shareholders are disposing of positions held.
- **Diversification:** Minimizes corporation's or individual's risk by investing in securities of several companies.
- **Dividend:** The amount of the corporate profits declared by the Board of Directors as a dividend to the stockholders.
- **Dollar-Cost Averaging:** Buying mutual funds or othersecurities on a regular basis with the same dollar investment. By investing on a regular basis, the average cost may be less than the average price over the same period of time.
- **Dow Jones Industrial Average (DJIA):** The DJIA is made up of 30 industrial stocks. The news networks use the DJIA to report the movements in the stock market. Throughout the day the value of the 30 industrial is added together and divided by a common divisor to arrive at the current DJIA.

- **Earned Income:** An individual's income from personal services. Examples include salaries, wages, and commissions.
- **Economic Indicators:** Statistical data identifying the current direction f the economy. There are leading, coincident and lagging indicators.
- **Ecliptic a collection of, to gather together.**
- **Effective Date:** The date sales of a security offering begins security registration effective.
- **Equity:** is Ownership. Common and preferred stockholders have equity positions in a corporation. The amount of ownership the customer has in the margin account. Also, total assets minus total liabilities equals equity.
- **ERISA:** Employee Retirement Income Securities Act. Passed in 1972 to set standards for the retirement plans. The act requires that plan assets be managed and administered prudently so that employees will be assured of retirement benefits.
- **Estate tax:** The amount of tax due on a person's net worth at death.
- **Exchange:** An exchange is central location where continuous auctions are held throughout each business day and the listed securities are sold to the highest bidder. Individuals buy a membership (seat) on the exchange and execute security transactions on the floor of the exchange for themselves and their customers.
- **Ex-dividend:** It means "without the dividend". Used to refer to a security that no longer has the right to receive the next dividend. An "x" will appear next to the name of the stock or fund to indicate that the share price has been reduced to reflect the value of the dividend. Securities include bonds, money market instruments, and preferred stock.
- **Executor:** a person who is appointed over another person's estate through the will of the deceased person (dies testate; decedent had written a will). The executor oversees the financial affairs of the deceased person.
- **Exempt Security:** A margin able security which is exempt from the Reg T requirements. Examples include: securities issued by the U.S. Government, securities issued by states or municipalities, listed nonconvertible debt securities and OTC margin able bonds. It also includes securities which are exempt from registration under the Securities Act of 1933. This includes private placements, U.S. Government securities, state, municipalities and non-profit organizations.
- **Exercise Price:** See striking price.
- **Expense Guarantee:** An insurance company guarantees that increased annuity expenses will not decrease annuity payments.
- **Expense Ratio:** The percentage of expenses to operate the fund in relation to the fund's net assets. The management fee is most of the fund's expenses. This ratio is an efficiency gauge for the fund.
- **Expenses:** The cost of operating the syndicate is deducted from the gross underwriting spread. This gross underwriting spread minus the expenses equals the gross underwriting profit. The gross underwriting profit is divided among the underwriting group.
- **Exponential:** Is the moving average in which the most recent prices are given more with in the average than earlier prices
- **Face Value:** the amount a bondholder receives at maturity. Interest is a percentage of the face value. Same as par value or principal amount.

- **Federal Reserve Board:** The Federal Reserve Board of Governors is located in Washington, D.C. It has nationwide jurisdiction and approves all FRD policies. The board consists of seven members appointed by the President of the United States with Senate approval.
- **Federal Reserve System:** Is a self-sustaining independent entity designed to regulate credit and the flow of money to produce a stable economy. Its purpose is to provide the country with an elastic currency and supervise the U.S. banking system providing a safer and more flexible monetary system. It's the nation's central bank and was created by the Federal Reserve Act of 1913.
- **Fiduciary:** a person or institution holding an asset (cash, securities, etc.) for another person and who has the authority to act for and in behalf of another person.
- **FIFO:** a method to determine which shares will be sold first (First in, first out). The first shares in (purchased) are the first shares out (sold). Also, FIFO applies to a business' inventory.
- **Financial Risk:** This risk is the uncertainty of the issuing company a business risk.
- **Firm Commitment:** The investment banker agrees to buy a corporation's entire issue of securities at a specific price. The investment banker (underwriter) is at risk for the unsold securities.
- **Firm Quote:** price of a security bought or sold on the inside market from a market maker.
- **Fixed Annuity:** annuity which has a fixed rate of return guaranteed by the insurance Co.
- **Fixed Assets:** Productive corporate assets that are used for a long period. This includes property, equipment, machinery, furniture and fixtures.
- **FLIP:** Family limited partnership. General partner and Limited partners in one partnership.
- **FLT:** Family living trust (testamentary trust).
- **401 (k) Plan:** This retirement plan is a supplement to a corporate profit-sharing plan and was named after the IRS code section 401. It allows a corporation to customize a retirement program to fit each employee's needs and also permits employees to contribute to their own retirement plan. There are two types of 401 (k) plans....salary reduction plans and cash or deferred arrangements.
- **403B Plan:** A retirement plan for University, civil government and not-for-profit employees. It has the same characteristics and benefits of a 401k.
- **529 Plan:** is a tax-advantaged investment vehicle in the United States designed to encourage saving for the future higher education expenses of a designated beneficiary. It is named after section 529 of the Internal Revenue Code. There can be significant state tax advantages and other benefits, such as matching grant and scholarship opportunities, protection from creditors and exemption from state financial aid calculations, for investors who invest in 529 plans within their state of residence.
- **457 Plan:** Tax code section 457 provides rules to govern all nonqualified deferred compensation plans of governmental employees and non-church controlled tax-exempt organizations. The pension plan designed to comply with theses rules is simply referred to as a Section 457 plan. Employees are allowed to defer compensation on a pre-tax basis though payroll deductions that further allows them to defer federal and sometimes state taxes until the assets are withdrawn.

Vocabulary

- **Fraud:** Intentional misrepresentation, concealment, or omission of the truth for the purpose of deception or manipulation.
- **Front-end Load:** A contractual plan in which fifty percent of the first year's payments goes for sales charges. Also, the front-end expenses incurred by a limited partnership to get organized and acquire the partnership's assets.
- **General Account:** Premiums for fixed annuities are credited to an insurance company's general account. This account invests in fixed income securities.
- **General Obligation Bond (GO):** A municipal bond backed by the general credit of the issuing organization. General obligation bonds are more secure than revenue bonds and thus trade with a slightly lower yield.
- **General Partner:** A person responsible for the debts and operations of the partnership.
- **Gift Tax:** A tax placed annually on all assets valued above certain dollar amounts when passed from one person to another.
- **Ginnie Mae Funds:** Most of the assets in these funds are invested in securities offered through the Government National Mortgage Association. The GNMA securities are backed by home mortgages and guaranteed by the Federal Government. However, the shares of a Ginnie Mae fund are not government guaranteed.
- **Good Delivery:** The seller must deliver to the buyer securities in good form. This includes: ownership being clearly stated, signature (s), round lots, no torn certificates and all other important information such as par value, interest rates, maturity dates, seal of the issuer, etc.
- **Government Security:** Any debt backed by a pool of mortgages guaranteed by the Government National Mortgage Association, with principal and interest payments made by homeowners "passed through" to the investor. Ginnie Mae's are the highest-yielding government-guaranteed securities.
- **GNMA:** Government National Mortgage Association. A government owned corporation authorized by congress and nicknamed "Ginnie Mae". GNMA issues mortgage-backed securities which are backed by the full faith and credit of the Federal Government and sell for $25,000. GNMA buys FHA and VA guaranteed mortgages.
- **Growth and Income Portfolio:** a portfolio consisting of growth stocks and otherstocks that have paid consistent dividends. The investment company's objective is to have both growth and income.
- **Growth Stock:** A common stock designed to appreciate in price; capital appreciation.
- **Hedge:** a hedge is a position on the bullish and the bearish side of the market. The one position is protected by the other position.
- **Hot Issue:** A security which trades at a premium in the secondary market.
- Immediate Annuity: annuity that begins paying income with a lump sum purchase.
- **In the Money:** A term used with option contracts when the underlying security has moved in price and the holder is in the money. A call is in the money when the stock price increases above the striking price. A put is in the money when the stock price decreases below the striking price.
- **Income Fund:** An investment company fund which is designed to generate income. Most of the assets are invested in bonds, preferred stocks and government securities.

- **Income Statement:** For an individual, it's a financial document that show the client's net income. The computation is: total income minus expenses equals net income (or net loss). For a corporation, it's a statement that shows the company's net income or net loss. The computation is: total income minus expenses equals net income or loss (NOI).
- **Index:** A benchmark that measure performance, such as Standard & Poor's 500 Index.
- **Index Option:** An option contract written on a market index such as the Standard and Poor's 500 index. An index is a measurement of the stock market and it's an indication of how the market is performing.
- **Industrial Revenue Bonds (IRB)/Industrial Development Bonds (IDB):** A bond backed by revenue from an industry that will create jobs for a municipality. The bonds are used to construct or purchase facilities to be leased or eventually purchased by the industrial company. For example, a power project or any corporation moving into a municipality that may qualify for industrial revenue bonds.
- **Inflation:** rise in prices for goods and services. When inflation & CPI increases.
- **Inflation Risk:** risk occurs when an investment doesn't earn enough interest to keep up.
- **Interest:** The rate of interest paid for using someone's money.
- **Interest Rate:** The interest rate printed on the bond certificate. It's a percentage of the bond's face value. It's also called the nominal rate or coupon rate.
- **Interest Rate Risk:** The risk of fluctuating interest rates market price of issued securities.
- **Interested Person:** A person who has a substantial interest in an investment company because of his/her financial interest or because his occupation is either directly or indirectly involved with the investment company. Examples include, a broker/dealer registered under the 1934 Act or an affiliated person and his/her immediate family members, or a person who has performed material services for the investment company.
- **Initial Public Offering (IPO):** A private company's first public offering of common stock.
- **In-The-Money:** A call option with a strike price below the underlying equity. A put option with a strike price above the underlying equity.
- **Investment Advisor:** A person under contract with an investment company to manage its portfolio. Also, a person who for compensation engages in the business of advising other, either directly or through publications or writings.
- **Investment Banker:** A firm that gives investment advice to issues and assists in raising long-term capital by marketing the issuer's securities.
- **Investment Company:** A company that invests other people's money in the stock market. This includes face amount certificate companies, unit investment trust and management companies (open-end and closed-end).
- **Investment Company Act of 1940:** This Act regulates the activities of investment companies. It also requires all investment companies that engage in interstate commerce to register with the SEC.
- **Investment Company Act Amendments of 1970:** This amendment to the 1940 requires investment companies to structure their sales charges, within the maximum limit, based on the services which they provide shareholders such as combination privilege, letter of intent, etc.

Vocabulary

- **Investment-Grade:** Bonds suitable for purchase by prudent investors. Standard and Poor's and Moody's Investors Service designate bonds in their top four categories as investment grade.
- **Investment Objective:** The client's purpose for investing in securities.
- **Investment Risk:** The uncertainty that the anticipated return on the security will not be reached.
- **Investment Tax Credit (ITC):** a credit against the amount of taxes owed the IRS. This is a dollar for dollar credit against a person's tax liability. Only certain types of property and research work qualify for the credit.
- **Individual Retirement Account (IRA):** A retirement plan that allows individuals to contribute money on a tax-deferred basis to a retirement account each year.
- **IRA Rollover:** When the assets in one IRA account are rolled over into another IRA account.
- **IRS:** The Internal Revenue Service, created in 1913 to administer the collection of Federal Income Taxes.
- **Issue:** Any type of security offering by an issuer or a previously offered security. A corporation could have several different issues of stock (stocks offered at different times).
- **Joint Account:** Two or more individuals who share in the profits and/or losses in an account.
- **Joint Tenants with Right of Survivorship (JTWROS):** A type of share ownership. Two or more shareholders jointly own shares. Each shareholder has an undivided interest in the total value of shares. Upon the death of one tenant, the shares pass to the survivors).
- **Jumbo CD:** A certificate of deposit issued by banks in accounts over one million dollars, generally paying higher rates of interest than smaller certificates. Jumbo certificates are a major investment of money market mutual funds.
- **Junk Bond:** Non-investment grade bonds, those with a credit rating of BB or lower.
- **Large-Cap:** A company whose total market capitalization is one billion or more.
- **Level Charge Plan:** A purchase plan in which the investor is charged the same sales charge each time a contribution or investment is made.
- **Life Annuity:** An annuity settlement option. The annuity payments are made for the life of the annuitant. When the annuitant dies, the payment cease and the insurance company keeps any unused benefits.
- **Limited Partner:** A passive partner in a limited partnership. A limited partner does not control the business of the partnership and his/her personal liability is limited to the amount invested in the limited partnership.
- **Limited Partnership:** A partnership which has tow classes of partners; at least one general partner and at least one limited partner. The general partner has an active role and manages the affairs of the partnership. The limited partners have a passive role and their liability is limited to informational tax return and all tax consequences pass through to the partners.
- **Limited Partnership Agreement:** This is a contract between the general and limited partners which specifies their rights, status and responsibilities. The agreement is more detailed than the certificate of limited partnership and may be separate from the certificate.

- **Liquidation:** Selling an investment for cash without loss of principal.
- **Liquidity:** The measure of the ability to easily turn assets into cash. An investor should be able to sell a liquid asset quickly with little effect on the price. Liquidity is a central objective of money market funds.
- **Load:** for mutual funds, it's the difference between the public offering price (POP_ and the net asset value (NAV). It's also called the sales charge.
- **Loan Agreement:** This agreement gives the broker/dealer the right to borrow securities out of a customer's margin account equal to hi/her debit balance. These stock loans provide securities for short sales.
- **"Long" Coupon:** An interest period on a bond for more than six months.
- **Long Term Capital Gain:** A capital asset held more than twelve months and sold at a gain.
- **Long Term Capital Loss:** A capital asset held more than twelve months and sold at a loss.
- **Long-Term Debt:** The issuer's debt which is due over a long-term period; more than one year.
- **Long-term Investment Strategy:** A strategy that responds to fundamental changes in the financial markets or the economy and ignores fads and day-to-day market–noise.
- **Lump-sum Distribution:** A single withdrawal of an account's entire value. Upon retirement, participants in an IRA or other qualified retirement plan can choose to receive a lump-sum distribution of the proceeds in their account. Certain lump-sum distribution qualify for special tax treatment.
- **M1:** This is a measurement equivalents commonly used in every day transactions to purchase good and services. The money you carry in your wallet is M1 used by the Federal Reserve to determine the money supply. It consists of cash and cash. This includes, coins, paper currency, checking accounts, etc.
- **M2:** This is a measurement used by the Federal Reserve to determine the money supply. It consists of funds which are convertible into cash and used to purchase goods and services. The money you carry in your wallet plus your savings accounts is M2. This includes all of M1 with the addition of: money market funds *mutual funds), etc.
- **M3:** This is a measurement used by the Federal Reserve to determine the money supply. The money you carry in your wallet, your savings accounts and time savings (money invested for a set period) is M3. This includes all of M1 and M2 with the addition of: time deposits for large amounts and re-purchase agreements which are held for more than one day.
- **Management Company:** The firm that organizes, manages, and administers a mutual fund, or an investment advisory firm which manages private funds.
- **Margin:** The use of borrowed money from a brokerage to buy additional securities.
- **Market:** The entire market where securities are traded.
- **Market Risk:** The risk exposure an investor assumes when the stock or bond is selling at a lower price and the investor is forced to liquidate.
- **Market Timing:** A strategy of buying or selling securities in anticipation of changes in market or economic conditions.

Vocabulary

- **Maturity Date:** The issuer's due date to pay the principal and any accrued interest on a bond to the bondholder.
- **Management Fee:** The fee which is paid to the managing group for supervising the syndicate during a security underwriting. This fee is included in the gross underwriting profit.
- **Money Market:** A term used when trading short-term debt securities (maturities of less than one year). This market is made up of dealers who have an inventory and actively trade money market instruments.
- **Money Market Fund:** A mutual fund that invest its portfolio in money market securities.
- **Money Market Instruments:** Examples of money market instruments include: bankers' acceptance commercial paper, negotiable certificates of deposit, and re-purchase agreements.
- **Money Market Portfolio:** A portfolio of money market instruments.
- **Moody's Investors Service:** an independent corporation that provides investment quality ratings for corporate bonds, notes and stocks. They also rate municipal short-term debt issues. This is the oldest and largest investment quality rating service.
- **Mortality Guarantee:** The insurance company guarantees mortality under life income options of annuities, which means the company will continue to make payments to the annuitant even if they exceed the owner's annuity contributions.
- **Mortgage-backed Securities:** Securities which are issued to the public and the capital is used to make loans to home buyers. As home owners make monthly mortgage payments the issuer usually passes-through the principal and interest to the investors on a monthly basis. These securities are issued by GNMA, FNMA, and FHLB.
- **Municipal Bond Insurance Association (MBIA):** A group of insurance companies that insure municipal bond issuers. The MBIA guarantees principal and interest if the issuer defaults. The ratings agencies give their highest ratings to insured bonds.
- **Municipal Securities Rulemaking Board (MSRB):** The MSRB is an independent, self-regulated organization that regulates the municipal bond industry to protect the public and the interest of the investors. It was established by the 1975 amendments to the Securities Exchange Act of 1934. MSRB regulates sales person, not issuers.
- **Mutual Fund:** An open-end investment company that has a continuous offering of shares and will redeem its shares. The assets in the mutual fund are managed by an investment advisor. The value of the fund's shares is determined by the net assets of the fund's portfolio. An investor owns shares in the mutual fund and the mutual fund owns the assets in its portfolio.
- **NASD:** Abbreviation for the National Association of Securities Dealers, Inc. NASD is a self- regulated organization (SRO) for the "over-the-counter" market. It does not issue capital stock; it's strictly a membership corporation. It's purpose is to standardize, problem solve and enforce the rules and regulations for the OTC securities industry.
- **NASDAQ:** A nationwide electronic system established by the NASD for price quotations and trading on "over the Counter stocks".
- **Net Asset Value (NAV):** the value the investor receives when redeeming (selling) mutual fund shares.
- **Net Income:** For an individual, it's gross income minus expenses equals net income. For a company, it's net sales minus cost of good sold and other expenses including taxes equals net income.

- **Net Profit Margin:** This ration tells a corporation what percent of every dollar in sales equals net profit. Net profit (net income after taxes) divided by net sales equals the net profit margin.
- **Net Worth:** For the net worth of an individual, the computation is: total assets minus total liabilities equals net worth. For the net worth of a corporation, the computation is: Total assets minus total liabilities (short-term and long term debt) equals stockholders' equity.
- **Non-Accredited Investor:** A person who does not meet certain net worth or income requirements and may be restricted from purchasing direct participation programs. Limitations are placed on the number of non-accredited investors in a program.
- **Non-Qualified Plan:** A retirement plan that does not meet IRS requirements, so there are no tax advantages when contributing into the plan.
- **Non-Qualified Plan:** A retirement plan that does not meet IRS requirements, so there are no tax advantages when contributing into the plan.
- **Offer:** The selling price of a security.
- **Offering Circular:** A document that explains a securities offering.
- **Open-end Investment Company:** The mutual fund, so called because it continuously offers new shares to the public. A new buyer purchases shares at the same price as all othershareholders at eh close of business on a given trading day.
- **Option:** The right to buy or sell a given security within a particular time at a specified price. The right to buy is a call; the right to sell is a put. An option does not obligate the investor to complete a transaction, only the right to do so.
- **OTC Option:** A option which is not listed on an exchange. These are traded among dealers in the OTC market.
- **Over-the-counter (OTC):** The market for securities that are not traded on an organized stock exchange, as ell as some listed securities traded off those exchanges. Most government, municipal, and corporate bonds are also traded over the counter.
- **Par Value:** The face value of a bond or stock as printed on the certificate. Bonds generally have a par value of $1,000.
- **Penny Stock:** Stocks in younger, relatively small companies. They carry more risk and sell for under $1.
- **Portfolio:** The security holding of an individual or corporation.
- **Portfolio Turnover:** a measure of the trading activity in a fund's portfolio of investments. The ratio of how frequently securities re both and sold by a mutual fund.
- **Preferred stock:** A class of stock with a fixed dividend that has preference over a company's common stock in the payment of dividends and the liquidation of assets.
- **Premium:** the price an investor pays the writer of an option above the option's intrinsic value. The amount paid in excess of par value for a bond or stock. The interest rate a bank charges on loans to its most creditworthy customers.
- **Prime Rate:** The rate set by the commercial banks at which their best corporate customer can borrow money.

- **Principal:** A dealer who invests his/her capital to buy securities or an investor who buys for his own account is acting in a principal capacity rather than an agency capacity. Also, the face amount on a bond is called principal.
- **Private Placement:** The sale of securities to limited number of investors at the initial stages of a company's operations, a private placement allows investors to invest in attractive companies before the company sells stock to the public.
- **Profit-taking:** Selling securities after they have risen in value to realize a gain.
- **Prospectus:** A Synopsis of the registration statement which provides the investor with the material information necessary to make an informed decision on new issues. The registration sta4ement is filed with the SEC.
- **Proxy:** A written authorization that allows one person to act for another. For example, shareholders who are unable to attend a fund's annual meeting may mail in their ballots and vote by proxy.
- **Prudent Man Rule:** The legal foundation for professional investment management, which requires one who controls funds for others to act solely for the benefit of the client.
- **Public Offering Price (POP):** The purchase price of one share of an open-end mutual fund, including the sales charge. The POP is equal to the NAV plus the sales charge.
- **Qualified Retirement Plan:** A retirement plan that meets the IRS requirements. Certain tax advantages are only available on qualified retirement plans.
- **Real rate of return:** The return on an investment after it is adjusted for the effects of time.
- **Record Date:** The date that determines which shareholders will be paid the dividend or capital gain declared by a corporation or mutual fund. Only shareholders who are invested at the opening of business on the record date will receive the distribution.
- **Redemption:** the process of converting shares into cash. Any open-end mutual fund must redeem shares at the current price from a registered shareholder upon request.
- **Reinvestment privilege:** The right of shareholders to use income and/or capital gain distributions to purchase additional shares of their fund without paying a sales charge.
- **Revenue Bond:** A municipal bond that is backed by the revenue from the project being financed. Revenue bonds are less securely backed than general obligation bonds, and thus may trade with higher yields.
- **Rights of accumulation (ROA):** A way for a shareholder to qualify for a reduced sales charge by adding the value of shares already owned in the accounts to the amount of a new purchase. Also referred to as cumulative quantity discount.
- **Roth-IRA:** A qualified plan where contributions are not tax-deductible but distributions are tax-free if certain specified conditions are met.
- **Royalty Interest:** The owner of the oil and gas mineral rights has a royalty interest in the production. The owner does not pay any of the production costs, but only benefits if the property produces.
- **Sales Charge:** All charges and fees that are described in the prospectus as sales related expenses. This includes front-end or initial charges, asset-based charges, and contingent deferred or redemption charges. A front-end charge is the difference between the NAV and the POP when buying mutual funds or the sales charge when purchasing variable annuities.

Vocabulary

- **Securities and Exchange Commission (SEC):** The Federal agency created by the Securities and Exchange Act of 1934 that administers the laws governing the securities markets. The SEC regulates the registration and distribution of mutual funds shares.
- **Self-directed retirement account:** A retirement account offered through an investment dealer that can include stock, bonds, and mutual funds. S called because the investors are free to make their own investment decisions.
- **Share:** A unit of ownership in a fund or corporation.
- **Shareholder:** An owner of shares of a mutual fund or corporation.
- SEP-IRA: A qualified retirement plan for small businesses with 25 or fewer employees.
- **Standard deviation:** The measurement of the average difference between a portfolio's periodic returns and a benchmark index. The smaller the difference, the lower the standard deviation and the more stability in price movements.
- **Standard and Poor's Corporation:** This corporation provides investment quality ratings for debt securities, equity securities and commercial paper. They also compile several index like the S&P 500 and the S&
- **Standard and Poor's 500:** An index is a weighted average of the stock market and gives a measurement of how the market is performing. This index is compiled by the Standard and Poor's and includes 400 industrial companies, 20 transportation, 40 financial and 40 public utilities.
- **Stock Certificate:** A Written certificate which verifies ownership in the corporation and also shows the number of shares owned by the holder of such certificate.
- **Stock Dividend:** The board of directors declares additional shares in the corporation to the common stockholders as a stock dividend.
- **Stock Split:** A stock split is declared by the corporation's board of directors. A Stock split "up" will increase the number of shares the investor owns in the corporation, but decrease the market price per share. A stock split "down" will decrease the number of shares the investor owns in the corporation, but increase the market price per share. The stockholders have the same equity after the split as they did before the split.
- **Striking (Exercise) Price:** The price at which the holder of the option can buy stock (call) from the write or sell stock- put) to the writer.
- **Tax Basis:** It's an accounting procedure to determine the amount of money the client could lose in the investment. The tax basis is the limit for eligible deductions. An investor cannot write off more than his/her tax basis.
- **Tax Deferred:** Income whose taxes can be postponed until a later date. Contributions to a 401k plan, for example, are not taxed until they are withdrawn from the account, but when withdrawn, they are fully taxed at the applicable tax rate for ordinary income. Withdrawals made from a 401k plan before age 59 ½ may also be subject to a 10% IRS penalty.
- **Tax-exempt security:** A municipal bond. A security whose current income is not subject to current tax.
- **Tax loss carry-forward:** A tax benefit that allows an individual or a mutual fund to offset past losses against future profits. Technical analysis of the supply and demand for securities using charts and graphs to identify price trends that may foretell future price movements.

Vocabulary

- **Tenants in Common:** Two or more individuals who own an interest in some asset. At the death of one tenant, his/her interest goes to whomever he/she designates.
- **Tender Offer:** An offer by a wealthy investor or group of investors to buy the current stockholders' shares usually at premium price in order to take control of the company. Also the issuer or its current stockholders can make a tender offer to buy (or exchange, in the case of the issuer) stockholders' shares to reduce the outstanding shares.
- **Testamentary Trust:** A trust is a legal entity in which assets are placed. The trust assets are controlled by the trustee. The testamentary trust goes into effect after the death of the grantor. The grantor is the person who established the trust.
- **Total Return:** The return on investments which takes into account the change in price plus dividends or interest received. The total return for a fund and reflects changes in net asset value and reinvestment of all distributions in additional shares of the fund.
- **Transfer Agent:** A commercial bank or trust company selected by the issuer to transfer stock to the new owner. The transfer agent receives certificates with transfer instructions, cancels old certificates, issues new certificates and updated the issuer's stockholder of record book. For a mutual fund, it's the organization which performs the fund's bookkeeping duties which includes issuing shares, cancellation of redeemed shares, and disbursement of dividends and capital gains.
- **Treasury Bill (T Bill):** A short-term debt obligation of the federal government. They are issued by the federal reserve at weekly auctions throughout the country. T-bills are sold at a discount (less than $10,000) and mature at the face value ($10,000) generally within 91 days, but always within 1 year. The difference between the purchase price and maturity value is the investor's interest.
- **Treasury Bond:** A U.S. Government Bond which is issued at par, carries a stated interest rate and matures within 35 years.
- **Treasury Note:** A U.S. Government Note which is issued at par, carries a stated interest rate and matures within one to ten years.
- **Trust:** A trust is a legal entity in which assets are placed. A trust consists of the following three parties: first, a grantor who is the person that establishes the trust; second, the trustee which oversees and manages the according to the trust's instructions; third, a beneficiary who is the person that receives the benefits from the trust.
- **Trustee:** An organization or individual that serves as the fiduciary for one or more individual account, usually acting in conjunction with a commercial bank. The trustee is authorized to act on behalf of the accounts.
- **TSA:** Tax sheltered annuity
- **Turnaround:** a sharp, positive reversal in the performance of a company, industry, or the entire economy.
- **12b-1 Distribution Fee (Spread Fees):** This rule allows mutual funds to spread their distribution expenses over the years and deduct them from the asset so the fund. Distribution expenses include: advertising, marketing, advertising agencies, annual reports and prospectuses. This rule was approved by the Securities and Exchange Commission (SEC) in 1980 and named after one of its sections.
- **Uniform Gifts to Minor's Act (UGMA):** This permits minors to won securities. The account is managed by a custodian (a person of legal age) who buys and sells securities for the benefit of the minor. At majority (legal age), the minor receives the assets in the account.

Vocabulary

- **Variable Annuity:** An owner (purchaser) pays premiums into the insurance company's separate account. The account assets are invested in common stocks. The rate of return varies depending on the common stock performance. It's designed to keep up with inflation, although there is no guarantee.
- **Volatility:** the measurement of how much an underlying security fluctuates over a period of time.
- **Warrant:** A long term security which is similar to an option. A stock warrant usually allows a trader to purchase one share of stock at a fixed price for a certain period of time.
- **Wash Sale:** the sale and repurchase of the same asset within 30 days. The IRS does not allow an investor to claim a tax loss on a wash sale.
- **X:** appears next to a mutual fund's listing in the newspaper to indicate that the fund recently paid a capital gain or dividend. This amount was previously included in the fund's net asset value and is deducted from the net asset value when it is paid out. The "X" stands for ex- dividend.
- **Yield:** The rate at which a security distributes income, expressed as a percentage of the current price. For example, if a fund distributes $1 per share over the year and at the end of the year the price is $20, its yield is $1/$20, or 5%. Yield is an important measure of performance for income funds and individual bonds.
- **Zero Coupon Bond:** A security that pays no interest but is sold at a deep discount from face value. The holder receives the rate of return through the gradual appreciation of the security, which is redeemed at maturity for the full face value. Usually trades on a completely present value basis.

MONEY

Each and every year we face the Road of Life!

If we take the same road year after year we will always end up in the same place.
In January of each year we look down that road. We always make New Year's
resolutions, things like to lose weight, make more money, exercise or to make some
kind of changes in life.

We go down that road year after year from January to December. Hoping to find
the Path or turn that leads us to our secrets. The Secret path that leads us to Happiness,
Success, Love, Joy, Knowledge, Riches, and Peace.

As we return Year after Year, We notice that There were many turns and paths along
the way. Paths that you wished you would of, could of, and even should have gone
down, but we passed up that opportunity, that chance of successes and winning.

We now understand we can control our direction. It's our road and our choices the
directions we take. Our success is a right of our participation, and not just chance.
Don't take the chance that you would walk by and miss any of your wonderful
opportunities in life.

Plan your road, know your direction, take a helicopter view of your Road of life.
Look down and see where it goes and where the turns are now you see, where you
should of, could of, or will turn this time. Make it Happen take Control of Your life.

It's all about You!

Which Road
do I Take

www.ingramcontent.com/pod-product-compliance
Lightning Source LLC
Chambersburg PA
CBRC090836120626
46551CB00007B/679